9 9.77

edited by Doreen B. Massey, P. W. J. Batey · London papers in regional science 7 · a pion publication

alternative frameworks
for analysis

Pion Limited, 207 Brondesbury Park, London NW2 5JN

Printed in Great Britain

Contributors

J.Carney
*University of Durham,
Regional Policy Research Unit, Elvet Riverside 1,
Durham DH1 3LE*

M.Dear
*McMaster University, Department of Geography,
1280 Main Street West, Hamilton, Ontario L8S 4K1*

M.Goldberg
*Faculty of Commerce and Business Administration,
University of British Columbia, Vancouver,
British Columbia*

R.Hudson
*University of Durham,
Regional Policy Research Unit, Elvet Riverside 1,
Durham DH1 3LE*

W.Isard
*Department of Regional Science,
University of Pennsylvania, Philadelphia,
Pennsylvania 19174*

J-P.Laurençin
*Institut de Recherche Économique et de
Planification, Grenoble*

R.Lee
*Department of Geography, Queen Mary College,
University of London, Mile End Road,
London E1 4NS*

J.Lewis
*Department of Geography,
University of Cambridge, Cambridge CB2 3EN*

Oonagh McDonald MP
*Houses of Parliament, Westminster,
London SW1A OAA*

J-C.Monateri
*Institut de Recherche Économique et de
Planification, Grenoble*

P.Nijkamp
*Faculty of Economic Science, Free University,
Amsterdam*

C.Palloix
*Institut de Recherche Économique et de
Planification, Grenoble*

S.H.Putman
*Department of City and Regional Planning,
University of Pennsylvania, Philadelphia,
Pennsylvania 19174*

B.Secchi
*Urbanistica dell'Istituto Universitario di
Architettura, Venice*

R.Tiberghien
*Institute de Recherche Économique et de
Planification, Grenoble*

P.Vernet
*Institut de Recherche Économique et de
Planification, Grenoble*

Contents

Introduction

This issue of *London Papers* contains selections from two separate Regional Science Conferences, both of which were held in London during 1975. The first selection, and the one to which this note is primarily an introduction, consists of papers from the third annual meeting of the North West European Multilingual RSA (the unpronounceable NWEMRSA!)[1]. The second set is from the conference normally recorded in *London Papers*, that of the annual meeting of the British Section.

Johnston (1976), in his review of *London Papers 6*, commented that "the progress of the discipline of regional science can be charted through the publications of the conference papers of the main body and of the various branches of the Regional Science Association". The juxtaposition of the two groups of papers in this volume is an illustration of the particularly challenging nature of 'progress' at the present time. Thus NWEMRSA itself was founded, with the backing of the international RSA, in an explicit attempt to break down not just linguistic and national barriers, but also some of the boundaries of regional science. In particular, an attempt was made to broaden the ideological and theoretical bases of the discipline as then established. The collection presented here represents the application of approaches, new to regional science, to the analysis of interregional relationships. The specific papers, and some of the issues raised, will be discussed at greater length below.

The set of papers from the eighth meeting of the British Section represents, in many ways, the more traditional preoccupations and methodological approaches of regional science. Thus the paper by Nijkamp develops a formal, quantitative framework for assessing the effect on spatial mobility of changes in environmental quality. Nijkamp demonstrates effectively the use that can be made of this framework by reference to a series of examples concerned with migration, tourism, and commuting in the Netherlands. Putman's paper falls within the general field of spatial-interaction modelling, an area of regional science which has retained the interest of many British Section members ever since the Section was formed eight years ago. The subject of the paper is the calibration of a Lowry-derived disaggregated residential-location model, and Putman makes the interesting point that, until recently, calibration has been a relatively neglected aspect of North American work in urban modelling: this contrasts sharply with the situation in Britain. Isard, a regular contributor to the *London Papers* series, takes as his theme hierarchical dynamics, and illustrates his new concepts by drawing upon

---

[1] The papers of the second (Louvain) conference were published in *Environment and Planning A* 7 (4).

some of his earlier work on the economic history of transport development in the United States.

In this selection also, however, two papers pose questions of the presently dominant methodologies: Goldberg is critical of some of the more recent approaches to urban simulation modelling. His paper is a welcome contribution to the debate surrounding the usefulness of urban models in decisionmaking and offers helpful advice to any regional scientists who may be contemplating building a model for use in planning practice. In the final paper in this set, Dear attempts to tackle the analysis of the spatial externalities of public-facility location by the use of a 'conflict paradigm'.

Unlike the papers from the British Section, those from NWEMRSA were presented to a conference built around a single theme—that of 'centre-periphery relations between regions'. Under this heading, attention was focused on the analysis of the structure of relations between dominant and peripheral regions. The conference was divided into three sections based on the spatial level of analysis. All three sections are represented in this selection. The first is that of the region in a world context, under which heading analysis focused on the effects on specific regions of major changes occurring in economic structure at a 'world' level. The paper by Laurençin et al. (the Grenoble paper) is from this group, and analyses the nature of apparent changes in the international division of labour, concentrating in particular on those resulting from the present shifts in the pattern and economics of oil production and the associated processing industries. This paper is a shortened, and translated, version of the one originally presented at the conference. At the second, or European, level, Lee's paper emphasises that changing structures of interregional relationships (and indeed spatial structure in general) must be understood as the product of the overall economic systems of which they are a part. This paper contains both a detailed critique of approaches to spatial structure (including that of 'traditional' regional science) which do not recognise the importance of the relationship, and an outline of a possible alternative approach, which uses data from the EEC. The final three papers examine interregional differentials and relationships within the context of the national economy—the third spatial level of analysis considered at the conference. Secchi argues that accounts of national economic development frequently underestimate the significance of the role played by spatial structure. He elaborates this relationship in detail for the case of Italy over the period since the late nineteenth century. Carney et al., in agreement with the argument of Secchi, approach the problem from the viewpoint of an individual region. They trace the progress of capital accumulation and of class relations involved in aspects of the formation of the North East as a depressed region of the United Kingdom. The final paper, by McDonald, considers the role of multinational companies in the creation and preservation of structures of regional inequality, and discusses the problem specifically in the context of the British case.

Apart from these themes of the conference, around which the papers were deliberately designed, a number of other threads of argument emerge from the NWEMRSA contributions. As already intimated, it is probably accepted by all the papers that spatial structure and the processes of economic development are integrally linked. In some cases, for instance the Grenoble paper, this is a fundamental assumption from which the subsequent analysis proceeds. In other cases the argument is presented explicitly, and the empirical work is in part presented as a demonstration of the proposition. What is interesting about this second category is the number of different ways in which the argument is presented. The clearest contrast is between the papers of Secchi and of Lee. Thus Secchi stresses that the role of spatial differentiation in national economic development is frequently underestimated, if not ignored. In other words, he is arguing that space may play an 'active role' in the processes of such development. In Secchi's paper this argument is conducted empirically in relation to Italy, where, among the industrialised nations, spatial differentiation has taken on a particularly acute form. The author stresses that the empirical content of his conclusions (that is, the *nature* of the relationship) cannot be generalised beyond countries with specified characteristics. The theoretical and analytical point (that is, the *fact* of a relationship), however, *is* a general one.

Lee approaches the problem from a different perspective. His argument attacks assumptions of autonomy, not of economic development from spatial structures, but of spatial structures themselves. His discussion concerns the way in which such structures are conceptualised—and argues that they cannot be explained simply in terms of themselves. The arguments of the two papers are to a large extent different sides of the same coin. The 'space' in Secchi's paper is not the formal and abstract distance costs of much geographical work, but spatial structure—itself the product of historical economic and political forces. Where the debate must continue is on the nature and extent of the 'active role' of spatial relationships in different historical circumstances.

Within the framework of this common acceptance of the relationship between economic and spatial structures, a number of different approaches are adopted. Most of them lie within the general terms of a Marxist framework; others do not. The contrast between the three papers posed at the level of intranational regional relations is instructive. Thus the McDonald paper was invited as a contribution with the specific purpose of discussing policy options for the labour movement in the face of a spatial inequality in part produced, and certainly exacerbated, by multinational corporations. The specific characteristics of this paper, in terms of the theoretical position adopted, are perhaps best illustrated by comparing its conceptualisation and analysis of the capitalist state with that of the two other papers. Both Secchi and Carney et al. analyse the state and state policies as an integral part of the development of national economic and spatial structures. In these analyses, the state is not above class relations, class conflict; it is both a reflection of them and is involved in them. It is therefore itself an object of analysis. In the approach used here by McDonald, the capitalist state is interpreted as being a structure which, unaltered but in the right hands, may be used as an instrument against the causes of regional disparities. The same theoretical difference may be seen in the distinction between capital*ism* and capital*ists*. The concept of 'countervailing power' adopted in the McDonald paper implicitly poses capitalists (or 'their' representatives) as the force to be overcome. In the analyses of the other two papers, it is capitalism which is the determining structure, which defines capital*ists*.

As well as different theoretical/ideological standpoints, the articles present a number of different aspects of the structure of relations between regions. The Grenoble paper discusses such relations primarily in terms of the spatial division of labour—in this case the international division of labour. The division of labour in this sense concerns production (both the differential location of different stages of production and the flows of commodities and capital which result), and the political, economic, and ideological relations between regions. Regional 'inequality' and spatial centralisation are specific facets of spatial organisation resulting from the operation of forms of the spatial division of labour under the dominance of the capitalist mode of production; both are treated by papers in this collection. Secchi's paper makes clear the link between the specific roles played by different regions in the Italian economy, and the persistence of regional inequality. The latter part of Lee's paper, on the other hand, concerns itself with the phenomenon of spatial centralisation. Both his paper and that by Carney et al. give some indication of mechanisms behind the process of spatial concentration under a dominant capitalist mode of production, but it is clear that much work yet needs to be done.

Finally, it is a central characteristic of these new approaches to the regional sciences that attention be paid to the analysis of present developments and changes, in this case in the field of relations between regions. The NWEMRSA papers in this volume are not engaged in the unearthing of the eternal laws of spatial structure. The existence of such laws is indeed rejected. The continuing development of the social and economic system produces new sets of structures, and new forms of the relationship of spatial patterns to that system. In that context, the Secchi, McDonald, and Grenoble papers, in particular, contribute to our understanding of the nature and role of spatial structures in the specific conditions of the present economic crisis.

The 'new' schools of thought must not be seen as constituting a single theoretical approach; nor one which can be provided 'ready made'.

Debate is as rife, and further work as important, as in all branches of regional science. Finally, every distinct theoretical approach has its own concepts and terminology, and these must be understood and grasped before any evaluation can be said to be adequate. It is a challenge which the originally nonmathematical amongst us, for example, have been taking on board for some time. It is hoped that this volume will stimulate serious enquiry into different theoretical fields, and that the juxtaposition of these two groups of papers may make clearer, and enliven, the terms of the debate.

Doreen B Massey
P W J Batey
London, October 1976

Reference

Johnston R J, 1976 "Review of *London Papers in Regional Science 6. Theory and Practice in Regional Science*" *Environment and Planning A* 8 605

The Regional Effects of the Crisis on the Forms of Organisation of Production and Location of Industry in the Mediterranean Basin

J-P.LAURENÇIN, J-C.MONATERI, C.PALLOIX, R.TIBERGHIEN, P.VERNET
Institut de Recherche Économique et de Planification, Grenoble

Introduction

An analysis of the current crisis of the developed capitalist economies requires one, as a preliminary measure, to define the scope and the 'organic' nature of that crisis. Thus we must first make quite clear the theoretical hypotheses related to the explanation of this crisis (this is done in the first part of the paper). In particular, it is argued that the common interpretation that the crisis is only one of the *regulation* of the capitalist mode of production, and not an organic crisis of capitalism, is inadequate for an analysis of medium and long-term effects.

The study of the effects of the crisis, and of its internationalisation in the Mediterranean Basin, particularly necessitates a more rigorous theoretical perspective. The Mediterranean region is a strategic moment in the reproduction of capital on an international scale, owing to the relationships which have developed there between economies of unequal levels of development—industrially developed and underdeveloped, dominant and dominated, oil-producing and not oil-producing. The study of the effects of the crisis in this region is the object of the second part of our paper. This study is not exhaustive and deals essentially with the countries of the South of the Mediterranean Basin, and with the Middle East. Finally, it should be stressed that the analysis is a sectoral one, and that the estimation of the effects of the crisis cuts across the various countries. The three sectors under study are: the equipment industry (mechanical and electrical construction); the iron and steel industry; and the petrochemical industries.

These sectors alone, of course, cannot explain the changes which are affecting the productive system of each national formation as a whole. It is clear that a study of the latter is indispensable for a proper understanding of the international division of labour when this is conceived in its full meaning, not only as the structuring of the productive forces, but also as the international organisation of social relations, where political and state action at a national level also play a role.

The crisis of capitalism and the international division of labour

The current crisis of capitalism is 'organic' because it affects the two submovements of capital: the process of valorisation, and the process of accumulation. Although the crisis might appear to be one of realisation (that is, of insufficient markets), accompanied by a falling rate of profit, this should not mask the deeper crisis of the conditions of the accumulation of capital. The crisis, in other words, is a crisis of the conditions of production of surplus value.

This crisis of valorisation[1] of capital is accompanied by the unequal development of industrial sectors, and the crisis of accumulation by an imbalance in the relations between productive departments. The analysis of the conditions of production of surplus value (relative surplus value in the advanced capitalist economies), or of variations in the rate of exploitation, should take as a starting point this division of the productive system. An understanding of the exchanges of value between the sector producing the means of production (department I) and the sector producing means of consumption (department II) is essential for analysing the formation of the rate of exploitation and the divisions between surplus labour and necessary labour, and between living labour (variable capital) and dead labour (constant capital).

The current crisis is organic because it affects the relations between these departments[2], that is because it affects the internal conditions of the accumulation of capital in the capitalist economies of Europe, Japan, and the USA. The relations between departments, which determine the development of the rate of surplus value, and through that the formation of the rate of profit, are at present confronted with the inability of department I to increase productivity in department II in order to lower the relative value of labour power. This is not only a technical inability: it is also political, economic, and social. The impact of the crisis on the international division of labour should be considered in this context.

Up until the present time, the international organisation of production has always consisted in allotting to the so-called underdeveloped countries the function of supplying the industrialised capitalist economies. Only the latter possess *all* the necessary elements for the organisation of production —in other words for the valorisation *and* the accumulation of capital.

This international organisation of production (or 'internationalisation of capitalist production') is characterised by the development of export

[1] The term *'valorisation'* denotes the process of the embodiment of value in the capital during its productive cycle through its successive forms as money, commodities, productive capital, commonodities, and money. This may be represented as:

$$M \to C \to P \to C' \to M'$$

where $(M' - M)$ designates the profit. Valorisation is thus related to the rate of profit, given a constant rate of exploitation.

'Accumulation', on the other hand, is related to changes in the rate of exploitation and to the production of surplus value.

[2] This analysis of the relations can be made more precise by breaking down further the division into departments. This is done in a study which IREP is at present undertaking of the departmental coherence of the internationalised national industrial systems of Great Britain, West Germany, Italy, and France.

industries in the underdeveloped economies. The division of whole sectors of industry on an international level, and the allocation of parts of a sector (for example, car assembly) to underdeveloped economies, constituted, and continues to constitute, a process of external valorisation, a process in its turn reflecting the problem of valorisation within the developed economies. Certain underdeveloped countries, such as Algeria, are starting to build up their own conditions for internal valorisation, but it remains extremely difficult for these countries to create the conditions necessary for the internal *accumulation* of capital within the international capitalist environment.

This present form of the international organisation of production is essentially what is at stake in the present crisis, in as much as the solution to the crisis no longer lies in the extension of the process of external valorisation but rather in the internationalisation of the conditions for internal accumulation of capital by the developed capitalist economies. The present 'internationalisation of capital' is a result of the need to deal with the crisis of accumulation, in other words of the need to put into order the relations between the two departments so as to restimulate the production of relative surplus value.

Two possible changes in the international division of labour may help account for the form of this process in the Mediterranean Basin:
1. The extension, by the developed capitalist economies, of relations of accumulation by means of the geographical extension of the area within which accumulation occurs to certain privileged parts of the underdeveloped zone. Thus, for example, the inclusion of Iran and Saudi Arabia in this extension, whilst other parts of this zone maintain the traditional function of supply.
2. The reduction of the accumulation area in the developed zone, with the continued development of the division of industrial sectors in the underdeveloped countries so as to increase the flow of external valorisation. After a certain period, however, this development, and particularly that of external valorisation, is dependent on the ability of department I to ensure the necessary geographical reallocation.

The effects of the crisis in the Mediterranean Basin
The equipment industry
The nature of the development of the equipment industries (mechanical and electrical engineering) at a global international level should not be allowed to conceal the tendencies of this industry at a regional level. An analysis of a number of countries should enable us to map out these tendencies.

In Italy and Spain, countries which both belong to the developed capitalist zone, the internationalisation of this sector continues to develop. Thus Spain, in particular functions, appears as a relay country (or staging post) for the very developed economies and for the multinational firms (ITT for example). The example of Italy is less clear cut. Mechanical engineering (unlike the electrical engineering sector) remains a predominantly national industry. Its development process takes place within the structure of the internal accumulation of capital. This does not mean, of course, that foreign capital is not present, but it does nonetheless put a brake on the process of locational change. Moreover, this process is also dependent on the need to solve the 'Italian problem', in other words the imbalance between the North and the South.

If we now turn to the countries of the south of the Mediterranean Basin, and of the Middle East, a double movement can be identified. On the one hand, there is an attempt to establish an equipment industry to serve as the basis for an autonomous national development, and on the other hand there is the evident integration of these countries into the international capitalist system.

These movements affect the countries under study unequally, and it is necessary to make a distinction between the countries on this basis.

The first group of countries includes Algeria, Iraq and Iran. Here the first movement is the dominant tendency. These three countries, and in particular Algeria and Iran, have started important projects in this sector, in liaison with the projected development of the other industrial sectors. Quite apart from the use of foreign engineering skills and minor share participation by foreign firms, these countries' control over their industrial development is dependent upon the establishment of the conditions necessary for the national accumulation of capital. This in turn raises the question of whether or not the organisation of adequate relations between the two departments on a national basis must imply a break with the world capitalist system. On this point Algeria and Iran seem to have different responses, the two movements mentioned above apparently being in a state of equilibrium at the present time in Iran.

The second group of countries consists of Morocco, Tunisia, Egypt, and Syria. Here the second movement is clearly dominant. The nature of most of the development projects in these countries conforms to this second movement (they are mainly of auxiliary industries—sluice gates, boilermaking, etc), as does their orientation towards exports. These countries seem to be intent on providing industries, or parts of industries, which will ensure to the advanced capitalist countries the possibility of external valorisation and a more advanced internationalisation of production. The example of the duty-free zones in Egypt, and of the investment projects of Iran in these zones, illustrates the possibility of a triangular mechanism of external valorisation, a coherent mechanism expressing the latent inequalities in political and economic power within the zone of the 'peripheral countries'. The existence of a national basis for capital accumulation, and the type of departmental coherence which characterises this basis, will be decisive in determining the relations of domination which are established, not only between advanced capitalist countries and the countries of the Mediterranean Basin, but also among the Mediterranean Basin countries themselves.

The iron and steel industry

A rapid survey of the productive capacities of the countries of the southern Mediterranean Basin [3] gives for 1974 a total capacity of about 2 million tons of steel. This level of capacity can not even cover the consumption of these countries. For the same group of countries, however, projects at present under way or under study amount to an additional productive capacity of 30 million tons of steel for 1980. The scope of these new projects, which for the most part were decided on in 1974, might suggest that a process of locational shift is under way in the iron and steel industry. Certain reservations should be made to this conclusion, however. First, this forecast capacity remains at a project level. Second, an analysis of the recent strategies of the large firms in this sector leads to the opposite conclusion, in other words that there is in fact a retreat of iron and steel production back into the developed capitalist countries. It seems hardly probable in any case that the developed countries will give up their control over a sector which is so essential for the accumulation of capital, both in the sphere of consumption goods and in the sphere of means of production. In this unstable context it is possible to isolate two types of development of the iron and steel industry in the countries of the Mediterranean Basin and of the Middle East. The examples of Algeria and Iran can be used to illustrate this conclusion more precisely.

In Algeria the project for the development of an iron and steel complex in the West puts into question the previous orientation of the strategy of the National Siderurgical Society (SNS), which essentially attempted to respond to national needs. The present state of technology requires the planned complex to be a coastal one. To be profitable, such a complex requires a minimum output of 10 million tons a year. Thus in 1985 Algeria will have a total capacity of 12 million tons a year, of which about 5 million tons will be absorbed by the internal market. This in turn will result in a considerable degree of dependence on the world market, in spite of the fact that the new orientation to the exterior will be integrated into an industrial plan intended to guarantee national economic independence.

Iran, by 1983, is expected to have a home consumption of 12 million tons, and a productive capacity, after the completion of the large number of projected developments, of 17 million tons. These 'official' estimates must be treated with caution, and in particular may overestimate internal demand; certainly a large number of projects are planned. A notable feature of these projects is the participation in the capital of NISIC (National Iranian Steel Industries Co.) of those who control the processes.

[3] The countries concerned are Kuwait, Iran, and the countries of the Arab Iron and Steel Union: Mauritania, Morocco, Algeria, Tunisia, Libya, Egypt, Sudan, Saudi Arabia, Syria, Lebanon, Jordan, Iraq.

In other words, the development of the iron and steel sector in Iran seems from the very outset to be conceived as being closely tied in with the dominant firms and markets at the international level.

The petrochemicals industry

The organic-chemical industry, an industry which is primarily based on hydrocarbons, is at present undergoing structural changes. These changes are in part a result of the crisis in the industrialised capitalist economies as a whole. The birth and development of the petrochemical industry, from 1950 to 1975, took place within these industrialised economies. It is, however, possible that significant changes in the structure of production and exchange, and also in geographical location, may result from the recent development of petrochemical production in a number of other areas of the world. Among other regions, the Mediterranean Basin, and especially the oil-producing countries of the Middle East and North Africa, are in a particularly advantageous position for the potential development of the petrochemical and gas industry.

One hypothesis intended to explain these new tendencies in the Mediterranean Basin consists in suggesting that they are due partly to the autonomous decisions of the countries concerned and partly to the structural and sectoral effects of the crisis in the 'centre' countries, which in turn is leading to a new process of international restructuring within the petrochemical industry. The primary evidence of this restructuring is the tendency towards the reshaping of the international organisation of production and exchange in this industry. This takes the form of a significant but controlled transfer, over the medium term and the long

Table 1. Projected capacities for ethylene production: $(10^3 t\ a^{-1})$[a].

	1974		1980		1990	
	$10^3 t\ a^{-1}$	%	$10^3 t\ a^{-1}$	%	$10^3 t\ a^{-1}$	%
Industrialised capitalist countries	28600	85·4	45600	80	59500	65·4
New producing countries[b]	3100	9·2	7500	13	23500	25·8
Countries with a socialist economy	1800	5·4	4000	7	8000	8·8
Total	33500	100	57200	100	91000	100

[a] The figures in tables 1–3 were compiled from the following sources: *Chemical Economic Handbook* 1975; *Modern Plastics International* October 1975; *Informations Chimie* 1975 and 1976; *Economic Chemical News* 1975 and 1976; *Chemical Age* 1975 and 1976; *Hydrocarbon Processing* April 1976.
[b] This term covers all the countries likely to develop their own petrochemical and gas bases, including a number of developing countries. The main countries concerned are Mexico, Venezuela, Brazil, and Argentina (in Central and Latin America), Indonesia, South Korea, and Taiwan (in Southeast Asia), and Iran, Iraq, Quatar, Saudi Arabia, Egypt, Libya, and Algeria (in the Middle East and in North Africa).

term, of certain stages of production in the industry towards the so-called developing countries. Attempts have been made to classify the countries concerned on the basis of their productive petrochemical installations. According to such calculations, the capacities for ethylene production could evolve from 1974 to 1990 as in table 1. The 1980 figure can be further subdivided as in table 2, where a distinction is made between developing countries and other new producers. Analysis of the probable developments in the industry in the Common Market and in the Mediterranean Basin (including the Middle East and the countries of North Africa) highlights a set of tendencies which illustrate more clearly the conditions under which new forms of the international division of labour in the industry may evolve.

Table 2. Ethylene producing capacities in the new producing countries[a].

Regions	Certain projects		Projects under study	
	10^3t a^{-1}	%	10^3t a^{-1}	%
Middle East and North Africa	2876	38·2	4510	35·7
Central and Latin America	2080	27·6	1300	10·3
Southeast Asia	780	10·4	3650	28·9
Total: developing countries	5736	76·2	9460	74·9
Other new producing countries[b]	1805	23·8	3170	25·1
Total: new producing countries	7541	100	12630	100

[a] See footnote a, table 1.
[b] Amongst others: Spain, Turkey, Greece.

The structural features of the petrochemical industry in the countries of the Common Market
Within each of the different countries of the Common Market, production in the petrochemicals industry is structured in a relatively coherent fashion from basic products (olefins and aromatics) to the main derivatives. But this 'national coherence' within the industry's productive system is articulated at the level of the EEC under the dominance of the major oil and chemical companies and groups. This two-tiered structure leads to the formation of 'captive suborganisations' of production and exchange within the Common Market, a prime example of which is the network which organises the major exchanges between the localised petrochemical complexes of West Germany, Holland, and Belgium. This network links up a set of extremely important production locations in the Common Market, and in this respect it is possible to speak of a coordinated petrochemical industry in the North of the Common Market.

This captive organisation, or vertical integration, of production and exchange is related to the specific nature of the technico–economic process of production in this industry. In this industry, technical and economic organisation coincide inasmuch as it is the series of technical processes of production which make up the links in the chain of valorisation. Thus, each large economic unit within the industry is set up on the basis of technical processes which are all derived from the production and exchange of the basic products. During the period from 1955 to 1975, the growth (in terms of productive capacity) of the petrochemical industry in the Common Market has precisely consisted in building up the bases of the captive organisation of production and exchange. This physical growth has maintained a relative stability in the geographical location of the petrochemical complexes, a stability related primarily to the major refineries. Thus the geographical patterns of the spatial development of the petrochemical industry, and of the establishment of refineries, coincide during this period.

As already indicated, the setting up of such captive units was itself dependent on the institution of complex networks of filial or associated oil and chemical firms. The main multinational oil firms are well-established in these networks, as are also the large US chemical firms. Thus, up until 1975, the petrochemical sector in the Common Market countries constituted an extremely important industry. In 1975, the productive capacities for ethylene in the main industrialised countries and the forecasts for 1978–1980 are shown in table 3.

However, the situation has changed and new elements have appeared in the Mediterranean Basin. A variety of new strategies are being adopted with the aim of sectoral and intersectoral restructuring, and the petro-chemical industry is particularly implicated in this. However, the conditions of this restructuring appear to be contradictory in that they are determined by different decisionmaking centres and sometimes by divergent strategies. The strategic choices and decisions of multinational firms, those of a public nature made by individual states, and the growing number of 'mixed' projects between public and private sectors may be either mutually contradictory or mutually complementary. It is as yet difficult to trace clearly the different forms which such strategies will take. It does, however, seem that the forms and tendencies which have dominated the internationalisation of the industry up until 1973–1974 will have to be changed in the medium and long term.

Table 3. Productive capacities for ethylene in the main industrialised countries $(10^3 t\ a^{-1})$[a].

	1975 levels	Forecasts for 1978–1980
Common Market	11800	15900
USA	10600	15100
Japan	4000	6600
Total	26400	37600

[a] See footnote a, table 1.

New tendencies in the internationalisation of production and exchange in the petro-gazochemical industry

New producing countries: Algeria and Iran

In these two oil-producing countries, the establishment of the basis of a petro-gazochemical industry has been tied to the decisions made at the departmental level in the development plans and their strategies of industrialisation.

In Algeria, beginning with the 1st Plan (1970-1973) and within the framework of the department-level plan for industrialisation, it was decided to set up a hydrocarbon chemical derivative industry. Within

Table 4. Probable productive capacities in petro-gazochemicals in the countries of the Middle East and North Africa 1980-1990 (10^3t a^{-1}). (Source: *Economic Chemical News* 7 November 1975.)

		E	P	B	Be	Ox	pX	VCM/PVC	pE (ld)	pE (hd)	pP	S
Algeria	1	125						40	105			
	4	500	220	70	335		40	160				200
Kuwait	2	350							200			150
	4	500						200	250	100	50	
Saudi Arabia	2	500						125	200			125
	4	500						125	200	100		125
Egypt	2	300	150	50	155	50	70	110	170		100	90
	4	500	220	70				150	200			100
Iraq	2	150						65	60	30		
	4	500								100	100	
Abu Dhabi	2	400						200	150	190		
Tunisia	2	350							150			
Quatar	2	300							150	50		
Libya	3	350							150			
Syria	3	350							150			
Dubai	3	350							150			
Other projects					160	80	100					
Total		6025	590	190	650	130	210	1175	2285	570	250	790

Key

Basic products
E is ethylene
P is propylene
B is butadiene
Be is benzene
Ox is oxylene
pX is polyxylene

Derivatives
VCM/PVC is vinyl chloride
pE (ld) is polyethylene (low density)
pE (hd) is polyethylene (high density)
pP is polypropylene
S is styrene

1 projects under way
2 confirmed (or almost definite projects)
3 projects under study: probable date around 1980
4 projects under study: probable date around 1980-1990

this industry, which was articulated directly towards national valorisation, pride of place was to be given to the gazochemical process. The second plan (1974–1977) is intended to build on the productive capability of the chemical industry, in particular by setting up a refining capacity.

Table 5. Summary of table 4: Confirmed or semidefinite projects (1 + 2) and projects under study (3 + 4). (Source: *Economic Chemical News* 7 November 1975.)

Projects	E	P	B	Be	Ox	pX	VCM/PVC	pE (ld)	pE (hd)	pP	S
1 + 2	2475	150	50	315	130	170	540	1185	270	100	365
3 + 4	3550	440	140	335		40	635	1100	300	150	425
Total	6025	590	190	650	130	210	1175	2285	570	250	790

Table 6. Productive capacities of ammonia in the countries of the Middle East and North Africa (10^3 t a^{-1}). (Sources: *Chimie Actualités* number 1526 13 March 1974; *Informations Chimie* number 140, number 149 January and November 1975; *Chemical Age* 12 March 1976.)

	Existing productive capacity	Projected capacity (up to 1980)	Projects under study
Algeria	330–340	540	365
Egypt	260–270	650	330
Iran	355–405	570	900
Kuwait	445–460	480	
Quatar	315–320	270	330
Saudi Arabia	210–215	270	1345
Syria	50	245	
Iraq	80	270	330
Libya		515	330
Tunisia		270	
Oman		490	330
Bahrein		260	330
Total	2045–2140	4830	4590

Table 7. Productive capacities of methanol in the Middle East and North African countries (10^3 t a^{-1}). (Source: *Chimie Actualités* number 1526 13 March 1974.)

	Existing capacities	Projected capacities (up to 1980)	Projects under study
Algeria		100–105	
Egypt		30–35	
Iran		660–680	
Libya		330–340	
Saudi Arabia		3300–3400	
Total in 1974	50	4420–4560	3030–3945

In this way, a whole range of basic products is made available, and the main processes of valorisation can be established.

For Iran, the decision to establish an industry based on oil-derivatives was taken in 1970, and the gazochemical processes was again given pride of place in the initial period. The similarities with Algeria are evident in terms of the choice of processes of production and the diversity of the projects. However the overall perspective appears to be different. Firstly the Iranian projects rely on a considerable degree of participation by foreign firms, in association with firms within the Iranian public sector; and secondly, the scale of these projects would seem to indicate an explicit preference for external markets.

Other countries
Other than in these countries, it is difficult to discern a clearly dominant tendency. In other countries, development is more a matter of a collection of projects (with the exception of Iraq, which is more similar to Algeria than to Iran), rather than the systematic establishment of productive bases which have their own internal coherence. In any case, this collection of projects (be they under way, or simply under study) indicates that a significant tendency towards the development of a petro–gazochemicals industry is already present. This in turn underlines the significance of the newly developing regions, and the specific importance of the Middle Eastern and North African countries compared with the traditional geographical bases of the industry. Tables 4–7 give an idea of the importance of the productive capacity presently planned for the main basic products (olefins, aromatics, ammonia, methanol), and for the principal derivatives, in the countries of the Middle East and North Africa for the period 1980–1990.

Significant elements in the new tendency towards the location of petro-chemical capacity in the Middle Eastern and North African countries
The setting up and development of refining, and the systematic exploitation of natural gas and associated processes (liquefaction lines in particular) are obvious signs of a change within the oil-producing countries in the valorisation of their oil resources. But, at the same time, these projects also reflect the necessary technical development of the petrochemical and gazochemical industry. Thus, for example, most of the projects are based on the projected construction of refineries or of liquefaction units (natural gas liquefaction) or the use of associated gas, and are the indispensable technological links in the chain of production processes.

The terms of the new international division of labour in the hydrocarbon chemical derivatives industry and its expression in the countries of the Middle East and of North Africa
It should be noted that the multinational oil and chemicals firms are present in many of the projects. These firms intervene in a variety of

ways, and exhibit the following characteristics, both separately and together: they may participate (to varying degrees) in the financial backing of productive investments, they may have direct access through their control of production to the extent of their financial participation in investment, and they may contribute to the supply of appropriate technologies and procedures both for the maintenance of installations and for the training of qualified staff. It is clear that most of the projects are export-oriented and, more specifically, that they are intended to supply the markets of the same foreign firms as are involved in financial backing.

To some extent these projects generate a 'specialisation' of production within the industry in the countries of this region: 'specialisation' in basic products, especially ethylene, ammonia, and methanol. This specialisation in predetermined segments of the industry illustrates the limits of the division of labour in this industry.

Contours and limits of the new division of labour

The segmentation of the industry is a result of the export capacities in the basic and refined products, which also limits the ability to set up derivative processes, both in terms of groupings of derivatives, and in terms of the scale of their production. The favoured derivatives are essentially polyvinyl chlorides and low-density polyethylene, these two being the most commonly produced of the range. This limitation to these few processes in its turn reinforces the technological dependence of the countries in terms both of the development of specific technologies and of the acquisition of particular types of equipment. Finally, these countries also lack any direct control over the trade networks and the major production markets, a situation which can, in the long run, cause productive over-capacity.

Adaptation or a new division of labour in the oil industry?

The question is thus as follows. Do the projects which we have studied in the Middle Eastern and North African countries, the productive structures of these countries, and particularly their degree of internal and external coherence, constitute merely a readaptation of the existing international division of labour, the main terms of which are the integration of these projects into the dominant networks of production and exchange in the industry in the industralised capitalist countries? Or, on the other hand, are these projects the first elements of a new international division of labour? The major pressures towards the latter result would be represented by agreements between producer countries to coordinate their investments, and by the search for market outlets other than the industrialised countries.

Given the present range of projects, it is difficult to see what the terms of such an alternative could be. Moreover, the tendencies towards an adaptation of the existing international division of labour in petrochemicals seem to be dominant in many of the projects in most countries of the region.

Regional Relations and Economic Structure in the EEC [†]

R LEE
Queen Mary College, University of London

Introduction
This paper is an initial attempt to demonstrate the determinant relationship between economic structure and regional relations. Its underlying theme is the nature and significance of spatial structures within a capitalist economy, and its objective is to question the assumption of the autonomy and independence of space and regional relations in regional science. It has four major sections. The first presents the major argument and issues of the paper and is followed by two sections which set out an outline and critique of recent neoclassical studies of regional inequality in the European Community. The final section traces an alternative approach and presents, in a highly tentative fashion, some empirical material with which to illustrate the argument.

Spatial structure as ideology
Regional inequality within the economy of the EEC is frequently presented as a matter of some autonomous significance. Thus the various heads of state of the original six member countries, for example, were at pains to assure their subjects that in creating the EEC they were "anxious to strengthen the unity of their economies and to ensure their harmonious development by reducing the differences existing between the various regions and by mitigating the backwardness of the less favoured" (Preamble: Treaty of Rome). This sort of concern with regional inequality serves the ideological level of the social formations in Western Europe. The stress on national economic unity deliberately obscures the class structure of European capitalism (for example Westergaard and Resler, 1975), and the emphasis on regions translates this class-structural issue into a technical matter of regional imbalance.

In fact analyses of regional relations stand in great danger of isolating regional 'problems' from the structure of the economy as a whole. Policy measures can then be diverted from the internal characteristics of capitalist economies towards regional 'solutions' which isolate cause and effect. An example of this tendency is the separation of the EEC's industrial policy (for which there is no call in the Treaty of Rome) from its regional policy, and the placing of regional policy within the context of economic

[†] This paper is complementary to another (Lee, 1976a) which discusses the nature of integration within the EEC. Although use is made of the empirical material in both papers, the substantive content of each is quite different and could not be incorporated in a cohesive fashion within one paper.

and monetary union. The reasons for this are that (1) regional inequality is viewed as a problem of a laggardly market mechanism (see below) rather than as the spatial manifestation of processes of structural centralization and the resultant locational concentration of capital in the EEC; and that (2) the structural basis of economic and monetary union is itself poorly understood (cf Poulantzas, 1974), being perceived as a framework for supranational state intervention and as a means, in part, of solving regional problems by the transfer of resources from developed to underdeveloped regions[1]. In this way the objective facts that the appropriation of nature in complex industrial societies (capitalist or socialist) imposes certain locational imperatives, involving the production of regional inequality via large-scale industrial and urban production, and that in capitalist economies accumulation necessitates structural centralization, which in turn produces locational concentration, are sidestepped and ignored. Exchange relations, not production relations, are the objectives of capitalist economic policy and yet it is the relations of production which underlie regional relations (Lee, 1976a).

So regional issues are not autonomous; they are very much those of class and social structure. Geographical space does affect the distribution of real income (Harvey, 1973) but it is hardly effective in the allocational structure (the processes and institutions of resource allocation and the dynamic which structures their operation) within the capitalist mode of production. Power-centralizing institutions, such as private ownership, an increasingly concentrated structure of capital, and state planning in the face of the dynamics of intermetropolitan competition, are the crucial forces, and in this context space is both inert and insignificant. Thus the failure of socialists to study the spatial dimension of inequality in a market economy (Holland, 1975) is not serious if the objective is to uncover the structural bases of inequality. If, however, the object is to document the nature of distributional inequality (inequality in the distribution of real income) location as a factor has some relevance (Chisholm, 1971; Coates and Rawstron, 1971). Even then spatial variation (of, for example, employment and income) is hardly an independent variable. It is determined by concentrated allocation processes within the contemporary capitalist economy. In fact the spatial structure of society is simply the "spatial form of organization adopted by the industrial economy to achieve its growth goals" (Richardson, 1972, page 29). A corollary of this argument is significant. Whereas it is true that spatial organization may respond to all kinds of private and public industrial policy and action, it is wrong to argue inversely that spatial strategies can be used to modify the allocational structure of industrial capitalism—even if some distributional modifications can be achieved.

[1] See, for example, Point 5, *Final communiqué*, Conference of Heads of State or Government, Paris, October, 1972; Magnifico (1973); Denton (1974); Dennis and Presley (1976).

Regional economic relations then are the spatial expression of the dominant mode of production. To understand them it is necessary to understand that mode (Lee, 1976a), and if this is so the scale and location of regional relations are niceties of detail rather than fundamental issues. It is necessary therefore in any investigation of the spatial structure of capitalist society to place its lack of autonomy and its ideological properties at the heart of the analysis. An initial attempt to undertake such a task in empirical terms is made below, but first some alternative approaches to the study of regional relations which accept the autonomy of spatial structure and neglect its ideological function are discussed.

The nature of regional relations in neoclassical analysis

The major deficiencies of the neoclassical mode of analysis derive from its idealized conceptualization of the economy as a series of mechanistic encounters between flows of money and goods and factors (for example Hodder and Lee, 1974). Socially anaesthetized households and firms are considered only as market agents, not as part of a social structure. Conflict is replaced by consensus and the markets ensure an automatic, though interruptible, tendency towards equilibrium. So no special attention is paid to the unidirectional dynamics of capitalism which enforce a continuous process of accumulation. Thus, within the neoclassical system, economic activity is essentially static. There is no underlying driving force because the satisfaction of consumer demand is assumed to be the overriding objective, and the economic problem is an organizational one—that of matching ends and scarce means which have alternative uses. The notion that the economic dynamic is distinctively capitalist and necessary to the capitalist mode of production does not enter into such analyses. Indeed it is questionable whether or not neoclassically based analyses of the economy even recognize capitalism as a particular social form, as their analyses exclude its basic features and their policy prescriptions implicitly assume the desirability of its continued existence.

It follows from such analyses that relations between spatially defined parts of economies (regions) are simply summations of the individual market relationships existing between and within groups of firms and households. (So in neoclassical analyses, too, the existence of regions as objects is highly questionable.) The relationships between regions are adjustable by either a change in their content of households and firms or by a modification of their market position relative to each other. These alternatives are not mutually exclusive—capital may be moved from high- to low-cost labour areas and so effect an adjustment on both counts—and they may both be achieved by public and private means. Furthermore, as a result of the lack of attention given to the particular allocation conditions of capitalism, the regional problem is usually conceived of in distributional, rather than in allocational terms. Thus the EEC's "regional problem" has been defined as "discrepancies in living standards, job opportunities and social conditions between regions" (Thirlwall, 1974, page 112).

The nature of regional relations in the EEC: two views
Recent neoclassical analyses of regional relations within the EEC adopt a location and scale-specific approach. They conceive of relations at two scales—existing intranational relations and developing international relations—which result from increased integration within the EEC. But such a distinction is based upon scale differences rather than upon the political significance of further integration. Indeed neoclassical studies undertake no discussion of the relationship between the nation-state and the internationalization of capitalist relations and so it follows that economic and monetary union merely represents a change in scale as the member countries are already internal common markets. And yet, despite this distortion by simplification of economic reality, conventional economic theory is considered by one commentator to be "not much of a guide as to what might happen" (Thirlwall, 1974, page 110) at the new scale.

In neoclassical analyses the market—responding to the conditions of demand and to regional supply conditions (not dynamic economy-wide supply/allocation conditions)—governs regional relations. "At the root of changes in the economic geography of an advanced industrial society lies", according to Manners (1972, page 1), "the evolution of its consumer demands". This notion is, of course, quite consistent with the neoclassical view of the economy as an organizational system in which the 'evolution of consumer demands' is directly responsible for the evolution of industrial structure. Within the neoclassical economy, supply conditions have no autonomy either in the fundamental sense of structuring the economy or in the Galbraithian sense of guiding the economy in a preferred direction (Galbraith, 1974; see also Holland, 1975). So regional economic relations are determined by consumer demand, which structures the size and direction of the flow of purchasing power. This in turn involves regional effects, since industries are geographically specialized. Thus a switch in demand from, say, industries oriented to natural resources to manufacturing geared to markets, may be substantiated by the market process of cumulative causation and endogenous technical progress embodied in capital investment, which in turn is supposedly determined by the rate of growth of output. Looked at from this perspective, the evidence, for Great Britain at least, is "overwhelming that differences in the pressure of demand between regions is the major factor accounting for interregional differences in the percentage level of unemployment" (Thirlwall, 1974, page 114). Furthermore this process, it is argued (McCrone, 1969; Swann, 1975), will be exacerbated by the conditions of increased competition in an economically integrated EEC. According to this line of argument, regionally variable abilities (supply conditions) to sustain or attract an industrial structure governed by competition will be exposed by European integration and will aggravate regional disparities. Furthermore in a fully integrated economic union the operation of the principle of comparative advantage through exchange rates is no longer possible. As labour and capital increase in mobility throughout the integrated area, comparative advantage, which allows a region to produce those products for which it is most fitted, is replaced by absolute advantage which restricts the range of production options open to the region to those products which can be produced as efficiently there as in any other region of the integrated area.

Such interpretations place responsibility for regional uneven development upon the regions themselves: the victims are to blame. This is because within the neoclassical mode the economy is seen as an organizational system which sets in motion the various processes necessary to satisfy consumer demand. Certain regions simply do not have what it takes to supply these demands and so they are excluded in whole or in part from the transactions of economic activity. Furthermore the economy is viewed as a system of exchange relations, and conventional wisdom has it that regional equilibrium will be achieved through the operation of interregional demand and supply conditions. Such notions have been attacked from within the limits of exchange relations by writers such as Myrdal (1957) and Perroux (1961) who argued that uneven development is, in fact, an inherent and necessary result of competitive interaction. "Nonetheless, neither Myrdal nor Perroux, however progressive in admitting the inherent imbalance among firms, industries, and regions, grasped the force of the relation between structural concentration and spatial concentration as analysed by Marx in terms of labour reserves, capital accumulation, and the trend to monopoly domination" (Holland, 1976, page 39). In fact the role of labour migration, from reserves of labour in underdeveloped regions, in making possible a faster accumulation of capital in developed regions is an important part of Marx's analysis (1970 edition, chapter 25) of the accumulation process. And yet such notions are ignored by predictions (McCrone, 1969; Wise, 1963, page 137) that European integration will itself reinforce the "inexorable strength" of the locational centre. Such predictions are examples of a regional determinism which ignores structural conditions and emphasizes regional supply conditions. This is clearly demonstrated, for example, by the list of factors favouring the centre drawn up by Wise (1963, page 136), by the definition of the notion of economic potential in Western Europe and its supposed relationship with trends in industrial location (Clark et al., 1969) and, by the careful analysis of the role of location in the generation and maintenance of peripherality in the EEC (House, 1976). In fact the notion that integration will inevitably produce locational centralization has been attacked (Chisholm, 1964, page 11), but on the grounds of the assumed influence of individual decisions on labour mobility ("where labour *is* may be becoming less significant for industrial location, but where labour is willing to *go* may be becoming increasingly important"), whilst the structural relations between accumulation, locational structure, and labour migration are ignored.

Some of these issues may be confronted more directly by viewing regional variations from the point of view of the urban system[2]. Cities have been distinguished by their place in the corporate hierarchy of production, information flows, and decisionmaking (Goddard, 1974). Such a concept of spatial structure does bring the production structure of the economy into much closer relation to its spatial structure. But paradoxically a form of spatial determinism, which sees spatial structure as an autonomous object rather than as a dependent form (a notion derived from the technocratic neoclassical economy—see above), then argues that settlement structure is a mode through which spatial policy may be implemented. This ignores the fact that spatial structure is symptom, not cause, and so follows the ideology of contemporary spatial planning in capitalist economies (Lee, 1976b).

If spatial structure is considered as cause, then it is open to manipulation by planning to achieve desired goals. Spatial planning is by definition indirect, and is highly transparent (that is, the nature and extent of intervention are easily recognized), and so is ideologically well-suited to state intervention in capitalist economies. Thus it is argued, for example, that when the marginal regions have been "streamlined and equipped for European competition" (House, 1976, page 215) spread effects will outweigh backwash effects (an assumption incidentally of market power), and welfare may be diffused through the system simply by bringing the demand and supply for public and private goods into equilibrium through improved spatial access (see for example Shannon and Bashshur, 1974; Albaum, 1972). Furthermore the assumed dominance of spatial structure distorts the relationship between social justice and capitalism: as the capitalist mode of production does not enter the analysis, the apparent contradiction becomes that between social justice and economic growth. And this, for the spatial determinist, is no problem: "a principal objective for national-settlement policy would be to develop a pattern of urban units that would help the attainment of social objectives of equality of

[2] The space economy of the EEC is dominated by its urban system. No country, even the geographically most peripheral (Republic of Ireland) and least densely populated (France, Ireland, Denmark, Luxemburg), has an urban population of less than 50%. Indeed all but Italy and Ireland are over 60% urban, and West Germany, Denmark, and the UK are over 80% urban. Furthermore a central concentration zone in the EEC contains 90 million people or 35% of the population on 13% of the total area. Add the Paris region, Lombardy, and Liguria, and nearly 50% of the Community's population is located within 17% of its total area. Employment—a more direct measure of the spatial distribution of the economy—follows a similar pattern but GDP per capita is even more spatially selective, peaking around the capital city regions of Paris, Bonn, Brussels, and Copenhagen (Commission of the European Communities, 1973).

opportunity, while at the same time not being undesirable or unfeasible from an economic point of view". The reason that the diluted contradiction is no problem, apart from the dilution itself, is that "in the manipulation of *environment* through planning processes governments have a power to influence the achievement of not only economic but also social goals" (Goddard, 1974, pages 117, 115; present author's italics).

All of this is quite logical (but not necessarily correct) given that the argument is placed within the neoclassical concept of the economy and outside the capitalist mode of production. 'Environment' refers to a spatial environment, or to an economic system, in which the state has an assumed autonomous power to intervene. Under these conditions spatial policy can have a substantial effect and can be implemented by an independent and disinterested state. Reality is, however, somewhat different: the dominant capitalist mode of production in the EEC structures both space and the state (Lee, 1976a).

Viewed from outside the capitalist mode of production, the production hierarchy focuses attention upon the spatial organization of the tangible activities of the corporate economy and emphasizes the spatial dispersal, albeit unequal dispersal, of economic activity that results. At the same time it shifts attention away from the less tangible process of accumulation that such a structure has to accomplish. And with the continuing concentration of industry in the EEC (Commission of the European Communities, 1975; George and Ward, 1975) dependence upon the centre will also be increased. The structural and spatial concentration of industry involves, for example, an increased demand for goods and services from the centre, whereas an increasingly concentrated financial system, supported by an efficient hierarchy of borrowing institutions, leads to a corresponding export of capital from the periphery. This is, of course, an important element in the central underdevelopment of the periphery, since exchange relations are structurally determined to work to the advantage of the centre.

Arguments such as these have been advanced against the advisability of economic and monetary union in the EEC (Morgan, 1973), the reasoning being that nations would lose their ability to devalue their exchange rates. Others argue that this is a problem only in a partially integrated union. Full economic union could, it is maintained, be accompanied by a transnational regional policy which differentiates between high- and low-activity regions defined at the EEC rather than at the national level (Magnifico, 1973). Indeed the recent report on European union (Tindemans, 1976) advocates a two-tiered system in the Community. Such a policy would be financed by a European bank to be developed into a Community central banking system. Thus core and periphery would be institutionalized at the EEC scale. The direct flow of surplus value to the centre through the corporate hierarchy would be supplemented by flows resulting from the centralization of suprastate economic services. At the same time, a mechanism would have been devised to speed and expand the extraction of surplus value from the Community periphery in just the same way as the expansion of cities feeds the extraction mechanism at the local scale (Harvey, 1974).

Structural concentration and regional relations in the EEC
The argument of the previous sections may be summarized easily. Space is dominated by the mode of production; it has no autonomous power although it could be argued that spatial structure is not without effect in, for example, class structuring (see Smith, 1975). Regional relations within the EEC are simply the direct and indirect effects of an increasingly concentrated industrial structure. This structural concentration is accompanied both by locational concentration and by the imperialistic spatial extension of capitalism at a worldwide scale and by its structural extension within the urban system. Regional economic relations then are the spatial manifestation of material economic structures, and it follows that the spatial analysis of regional relations is subordinate to structural analysis and that spatial analysis may well distort and obfuscate fundamental structural conditions. Spatial structure is in fact a form created by the mode of production. It is a mere reflection of society as a whole.

The structural analysis of regional relations within a capitalist economy must begin with the spatial structure of the dominant units of production and with the accumulation process driven by competition. Even then the most that could be accomplished by such analyses would be (1) a statement that space is a medium in which capitalism operates and (2) a description of the various elements in contemporary capitalism's spatially extensive chain of surplus extracting, transmitting, and concentrating processes.

However, although space has no direct role to play in influencing capitalist relations of production, the spatial organization of production does induce spatial variations in distributional patterns. These derive essentially from the various levels of production within the corporate economy. As the concentration of industry has proceeded, centralization of control has accompanied the growth of the individual firms. The day-to-day management of production within individual branches requires coordination, whereas the planning goals of the firm set the framework within which production and coordination operate. The division of labour into these three levels operates with pronounced locational constraints. The production level becomes dispersed, in response to the pull of labour, markets, and raw materials, and it will tend to be more dispersed the larger the firm, with its increased power to command capital and technology and to plan production over a wide geographical scale. Coordination activities require white-collar workers, communications, and access to information, and so tend to concentrate in and around large cities. The planning function is even more concentrated, usually within the capital city, and needs rapid access to capital, government, and the media.

Applying this scheme to the world economy one would expect to find the highest offices of the major corporations concentrated in the world's major cities. Lower-level activities would be expected to be found in lower-order cities. In this way geographical specialization comes to reflect the hierarchy of corporate production, and the occupational distribution of labour in a city will depend upon its function in the international economic system (Hymer, 1972). Structural concentration will tend to increase the attractiveness of urban centres for high-order industrial functions whilst the periphery contains lower-order functions and accounts for a decreasing proportion of ownership and control of industry located within it. This provides another twist to peripheral underdevelopment as the centre becomes ever more highly organized and the periphery less and less able to organize itself. Peripheral disorganization is also promoted by growth-pole strategies which both tie the periphery more closely to the centre by articulating local urban structures, facilitating the extraction and concentration of surplus and adding to the flows from periphery to core, and impose a local redistribution of population within and between peripheral zones. This development is necessary to the process of capitalist accumulation (see above) and determines the spatial relations of production. So regional planning within the capitalist mode simply serves to facilitate the process.

The same forces determine the possibility of keeping surplus value within the region. "The order of possibilities of social retention of the surplus seems to favour the town rather than the country, the multifunctional town rather than the enclave, and the economic metropolis rather than the *entrepôt* towns or the local centres" (Santos, 1975, page 355). So in one sense industries retaining and capturing surplus value are indispensable in development poles; and public authorities, dominated by the idea of economic growth, would find it quite natural to make additional resources available to such areas. But it is not these areas that accumulate the surplus, and the possibility of the surplus value ultimately deserting the area would escape the believer in the efficacy of regional planning.

Centralization in the EEC city system
The city, or rather the system of cities, is a vital element in the process of European integration. From one standpoint the links between market, industrial, and urban subsystems are seen as "one of the clues of *European homogeneity*" and the town is regarded as "the expression, the fundamental structure and the essential channel of *European territory*" (Boudeville, 1974, pages 129, 130; present author's italics). From another standpoint "spatial integration in the economy, the evolution of price-fixing markets and the evolution of urbanism are inextricably interrelated through the necessity to create, mobilize and concentrate the social surplus" in a hierarchically ordered, global economy with "local centres dominating local

hinterlands, more important metropolitan centres dominating lesser centres, and all centres outside the communist nations being ultimately subordinate to the central metropolitan areas" (Harvey, 1973, pages 237, 262).

The distribution of large cities (measured by population, in both absolute and relative terms) is used here as an index[3] of spatial structure in the area of the EEC at three points in time (figure 1). These may be tentatively labelled as mercantilist, capitalist, and imperialist, as they correspond to historically definitive modes of production. They show how the distribution and number of world cities (that is spatial structure) in the EEC reflects the process of capitalist development from a local to a global scale and from a trading to a producing to a controlling function.

Two related features stand out from the maps—the dialectic between locational fluidity and stability in the set of largest cities and the trend towards locational centralization. During the three centuries to 1800 the most striking feature of urbanization was the growth of the larger towns to a new order of magnitude (Smith, 1967). By 1800 all the large towns were capital cities or ports with the exception of Lyons and, in fragmented Italy, Milan. Furthermore half the largest cities were located in the southern half of what is now the EEC, reflecting the significance of long-distance trading in the mercantilist era. The spatial extension of the mode of production and the increasing significance of the political level of the social formation provided the basis for this urban expansion. The evolution of regional and national markets, mercantilist economic policies, the growth of the nation state, and the centralization of government were major causal factors. A century later the situation was revolutionized. Coal-based industrial capitalism gave rise to large-scale urbanization in inland northern Europe and at the same time transformed the world pattern of big city urbanization by making Western Europe preeminent. Some elements of this spatial structure remained in 1968, but the major 'world cities' (Hall, 1966) of the EEC (London, Paris, Randstad, Ruhr), defined not only in terms of size but of functions which largely reflect their worldwide imperialistic role, are fewer in number and are all located within the northwestern 'golden triangle'.

The rapidity of nineteenth century urbanization and the subsequent concentration of economic significance in the capital cities provide two of the major reasons for the contemporary spatial pattern of underdevelopment within the EEC. So the evolution of the locational structure of big cities—viewed either as modes of European integration or as centres of accumulation and recirculation of social surplus product—provides a vital element in the structure of regional relations within the EEC. But the

---

[3] In the absence of any clear definition of capitalist spatial structure it is necessary to rely here upon fairly crude indices of urbanization which, it must be admitted, are concerned mainly with physical urbanization rather than its economic structure and so may be quite inappropriate.

evolution of the city system is the consequence, not the cause, of
economic development. Its spatial structure is a function of the hierarchical
structure of industrial and banking capital.

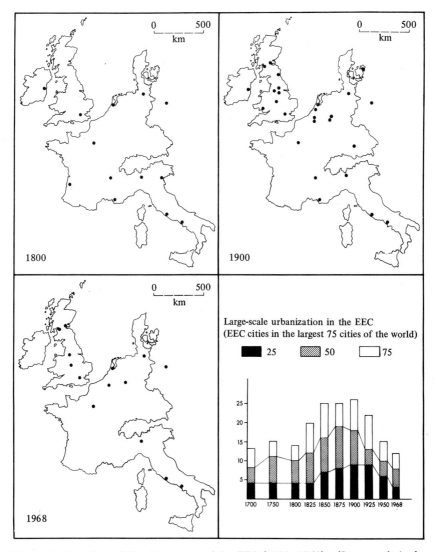

Figure 1. Evolution of the city system of the EEC (1800–1968). (Source: derived
from Chandler and Fox, 1974)

The location of industrial headquarters. "Cities", it is said, "are formed
through the geographic concentration of social surplus product" (Harvey,
1973, page 216). This being the case, the location of the economic
institutions designed to concentrate (as opposed to extract) the surplus
must play a decisive role in the articulation of the city system. Whereas
the location of industrial headquarters (figure 2) cannot be used as a
precise indicator of the location of surplus concentration, the fact that
they themselves show a marked degree of localization and that they are
closely associated with the institutions of banking capital (figures 3 and 4)
and other high level central functions of the capitalist economy (for example
Dunning and Morgan, 1971) suggests that they do give some indirect
indication of the location of institutional control of the surplus. Even
then it is the use to which the surplus is put and the implications of
concentration within the dynamic of capitalism which is significant in
allocation, although, as argued above, certain distributional consequences
follow from the locational concentration of the surplus.

Over 40% of the headquarters of the 500 largest industrial undertakings
within the EEC are located in seven cities (London, Paris, Hamburg,
Frankfurt, Munich, Essen, Milan). London and Paris together account for
over 30%. Furthermore the concentration is greater the larger the firm.
Thus London and Paris account for 40% of the headquarters of the largest
100 companies and 37% of the largest 250. Locational centralization
varies from country to country. France and the UK are clear examples of
a highly concentrated structure; Germany, with a comparable number of

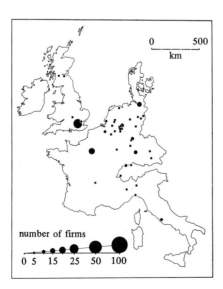

Figure 2. Industrial headquarters in the EEC in 1974 (100 largest firms). (Source:
Europe's 5000 largest companies Gower Press, Epping, 1975)

firms represented, is much more decentralized. But within the EEC as a whole locational centralization predominates, predictably within the central concentration zone. Furthermore the connection between the location of big industrial capital and banking capital both underlies the potential emergence of an EEC financial centre and structures regional economic relations.

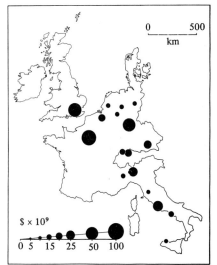 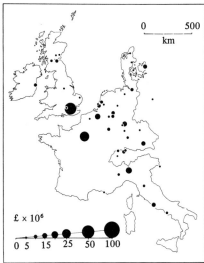

Figure 3. Banking assets in the EEC in 1973 (50 largest banks). (Source: *Vision* 15 December 1973, p 119)

Figure 4. Financial markets in the EEC in 1975. (Source: *Jane's Major Companies of Europe* Jane's Yearbooks, 1975)

The major financial centres. As in the wider analysis of regional relations (see above), it is possible to discern three approaches to the discussion of the location and evolution of financial centres: these include two market-based approaches and one structural mode of analysis. The demand for a centre's services may be assessed through the medium of invisible-trade statistics, or the supply conditions in the centre can be classified and described. But, according to Revell (1974), a more helpful starting point, especially in a dynamic analysis, is the nature of financial institutions and financial markets (figures 3 and 4). Support for this view comes from the comparative economic history of financial centres in the EEC. Thus the centralization process whereby London grew to be the dominant financial centre in Great Britain was inextricably linked with concentration in the financial institutions. It occurred through "failure, merger, or a change of headquarters" (Kindleberger, 1974, page 17). Similarly the postwar emergence of Frankfurt in West Germany was closely associated with the gradual reamalgamation of such institutions as the *Deutsche Bank* and the *Commerz Bank* of Hamburg which, in the process of centralization, both shifted their headquarters to Frankfurt. The situation in Italy is more fluid but shows the same processes at work. The mid-nineteenth century leadership of Turin was challenged by Florence and Rome and then, more significantly, from the late nineteenth century by competition from Milan and Genoa. Failures in Turin and Genoa then left Milan as the undisputed financial centre in Italy. Centralization in Paris was reestablished after the Revolution. Banks founded in the provinces (for example *Crédit Lyonnais*) spread out a local extractive network to concentrate the surplus not locally (for example in Lyons), but in Paris, even before the head office was moved there in 1882. Regional competition was removed by merger or driven under by the larger Paris-led firms, although *Crédit du Nord*, based on Lille, remained a regional bank and did not move its head office to Paris. Paris was also naturally favoured by various government institutions founded during the second half of the nineteenth century.

Contemporary structural changes in institutions and markets, resulting in a polarized size distribution in the former (Revell, 1973) and institutional domination of the latter, are serving to bind industrial and banking capital closer together and, as locational inertia is fortified by the increased efficiency of telecommunications, they (structural changes) will be the major factors in the process of international financial centralization (Revell, 1974; Kindleberger, 1974).

Concentration and localization in exchange
Although international variations do exist, there is a pronounced trend towards structural concentration in exchange. Between 1962 and the beginning of 1972 the number of retail establishments declined by 5% in the EEC (NEDO, 1973). Conversely the share of large-scale retailers in total retail trade is on the increase and forecast growth shows a marked increase in their share, especially in countries like Italy where they currently account for less than 10% of retail sales. In the UK by contrast they already account for over 50% of total retail trade and for between 20 and 30% elsewhere in the EEC. The degree of locational concentration of the headquarters of retail capital (figure 5) is not as marked as industrial and banking capital because several regionally based firms still rank high within the national areas of the EEC. But the same spatial pattern of concentration emerges, especially in nonfood, multiple-shop, and department store firms.

Exchange is of course one of the classical functions of central-place theory and has received far more attention than has the role of banking capital in city formation. But the emphasis has been on its role in the dissemination of goods rather than upon its role in accumulation. So cities are seen in conventional central-place theory as purveyors of development rather than underdevelopment. One of the reasons for this is that the object of analysis is the market elements themselves (for example the shop units) rather than the structure of their ownership.

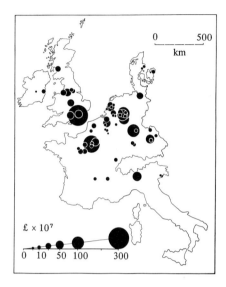

Figure 5. Headquarters of leading retail firms in the EEC in 1972. (Source: NEDO, 1973)

Conclusion

Structural and locational concentration in industrial, banking, and retail capital dominate the economy of the EEC and hence the regional economic relations within that economy. The latter are not the product of some independent, dynamic spatial logic and they cannot be reformed by a manipulation of that logic. The spatial patterns of production and the regional relations produced by them are simply particular dimensions of the process of capitalist accumulation and, although concentration produces a distinctive spatial form, that form is not especially significant in itself. So, in the context of European planning undertaken within the capitalist mode (for example Hayward and Watson, 1975), regional policy is inevitably supportive of that mode, both because it is designed not to address the process of accumulation and because it is concerned essentially with spatial responses to structural issues.

Acknowledgements. Particularly searching comments on this paper were made by Doreen Massey and David Smith and it is only to be hoped that their highly significant observations are as clear in secondhand form as they were at first hand.

References

Albaum M (Ed.), 1972 *Geography and Contemporary Issues* (John Wiley, Chichester)

Boudeville J R, 1974 "European integration, urban regions and medium-sized towns" in *Regional Policy and Planning for Europe* Ed. M Sant (Saxon House, D C Heath, Farnborough, Hants.) pp 129–156

Chandler T, Fox G, 1974 *3000 Years of Urban Growth* (Academic Press, New York)

Chisholm M, 1964 "Must we all live in south east England?" *Geography* **49** 1–14

Chisholm M, 1971 "A sociological portrait: location" *New Society* 25 November, 1029–1032

Clark C, Wilson F, Bradley J, 1969 "Industrial location and economic potential in western Europe" *Regional Studies* **3** 197–212

Coates B E, Rawstron E M, 1971 *Regional Variations in Britain* (Batsford, London)

Commission of the European Communities, 1973 *Report on Regional Problems in the Enlarged Community* com(73) 550 final (Commission of the European Communities, Brussels)

Commission of the European Communities, 1975 *Fourth Report on Competition Policy* (Commission of the European Communities, Brussels and Luxemburg)

Dennis G E J, Presley J R, 1976 "The national implications of economic and monetary union" in *Economy and Society in the EEC: Spatial Perspectives* Eds R Lee, P E Ogden (Saxon House, Teakfield, Farnborough, Hants.) pp 163–179

Denton G (Ed.), 1974 *Economic and Monetary Union in Europe* (Croom Helm, London)

Dunning J H, Morgan E V, 1971 *An Economic Study of the City of London* (University of Toronto Press, Toronto)

Galbraith J K, 1974 *Economics and the Public Purpose* (Andre Deutsch, London)

George K D, Ward T S, 1975 "The structure of industry in the EEC" OP-43, Department of Applied Economics, University of Cambridge, Cambridge, England

Goddard J B, 1974 "The national system of cities as a framework for urban and regional policy" in *Regional Policy and Planning for Europe* Ed. M Sant (Saxon House, D C Heath, Farnborough, Hants.) pp 101–127

Hall P, 1966 *The World Cities* (Hutchinson, London)

Harvey D, 1973 *Social Justice and the City* (Edward Arnold, London)

Harvey D, 1974 "Class-monopoly rent, finance capital and the urban revolution" *Regional Studies* **8** 239–255

Hayward J, Watson M, (Eds), 1975 *Planning, Politics and Public Policy: the British, French and Italian Experience* (Cambridge University Press, London)

Hodder B W, Lee R, 1974 *Economic Geography* (Methuen, London)

Holland S, 1975 *The Socialist Challenge* (Quartet Books, London)

Holland S, 1976 "Meso-economics, multinational capital and regional inequality" in *Economy and Society in the EEC: Spatial Perspectives* Eds R Lee, P E Ogden (Saxon House, Teakfield, Farnborough, Hants.) pp 38–62

House J W, 1976 "British marginal regions in the context of EEC policies" in *Economy and Society in the EEC: Spatial Perspectives* Eds R Lee, P E Ogden (Saxon House, Teakfield, Farnborough, Hants.) pp 194–216

Hymer S, 1972 "The multinational corporation and the law of uneven development" in *Economics and World Order from the 1970's to the 1990's* Ed. J Bhagwati (Collier Macmillan, London) pp 113–140

Kindleberger C P, 1974 *The Formation of Financial Centres: A Study in Economic History* Princeton Studies in International Finance 36, International Finance Section, Department of Economics, Princeton University, Princeton, NJ

Lee R, 1976a "Integration, spatial structure and the capitalist mode of production in the EEC" in *Economy and Society in the EEC: Spatial Perspectives* Eds R Lee, P E Ogden (Saxon House, Teakfield, Farnborough, Hants.) pp 11-37

Lee R, 1976b "Public finance and urban economy: some comments on spatial reformism" *Antipode* special issue on urban political economy (forthcoming)

Magnifico G, 1973 *European Monetary Unification* (Macmillan, London)

Manners G, 1972 "National perspectives" in *Regional Development in Britain* Eds G Manners, D Keeble, B Rodgers, K Warren (John Wiley, Chichester)

Marx K, 1970 edition *Capital* volume 1 (Lawrence and Wishart, London)

McCrone, G, 1969 "Regional policies in the European Communities" in *Economic Integration in Europe* Ed. G R Denton (Weidenfeld and Nicolson, London)

Morgan E V, 1973 "Regional problems and common currencies" *Lloyds Bank Review* **110** 19-30

Myrdal G, 1957 *Economic Theory and Underdeveloped Regions* (Duckworth, London)

NEDO, 1973 *The Distributive Trades in the Common Market* (HMSO, London)

Perroux F, 1961 "La firme motrice dans la région et la région motrice" Actes du colloque international de l'Institut de Science Économique de l'Université de Liège, Bruxelles

Poulantzas N, 1974 "Internationalization of capitalist relations and the nation state" *Economy and Society* **3** (2) 145-179

Revell J, 1973 *The British Financial System* (Macmillan, London)

Revell J, 1974 "Financial centres, financial institutions and economic change" in *The New Mercantilism* Ed. H G Johnson (Basil Blackwell, London) pp 74-89

Richardson H W, 1972 "Optimality in city size, systems of cities and urban policy: a sceptics view" *Urban Studies* **9** 29-48

Santos M, 1975 "Space and domination—a Marxist approach" *International Social Science Journal* **27** (2) 346-363

Shannon G W, Bashshur R, 1974 *Health Care Delivery Systems* (McGraw Hill, New York)

Smith C A, 1975 "Examining stratification through peasant marketing arrangements: an application of models from economic geography" *Man* **10** (1), 95-122

Smith C T, 1967 *An Historical Geography of Western Europe before 1800* (Longmans, Green, New York)

Swann D, 1975 *The Economics of the Common Market* (Penguin, Harmondsworth)

Thirlwall A P, 1974 "Regional economic disparities and regional policy in the Common Market" in *The New Mercantilism* Ed H G Johnson (Basil Blackwell, London) pp 104-125

Tindemans L, 1976 *The European Union: Report to the European Council (The Tindemans Report)* (Commission of the European Communities, Brussels)

Westergaard J, Resler H, 1975 *Class in a Capitalist Society: A Study of Contemporary Britain* (Heinemann, London)

Wise M J, 1963 "The Common Market and the changing geography of Europe" *Geography* **48** 129-138

Central and Peripheral Regions in a Process of Economic Development: The Italian Case

B.SECCHI
Istituto Universitario di Architettura di Venezia

Introduction

The main subject of these notes is Italian economic development during the period between the immediate postwar years and 1970. The primary hypothesis is that in the interpretation of the events of that period, in the development as well as in the crisis of the Italian economic system, the role of geography is less marginal than is usually assumed. Among the geographical problems, those which should receive the greatest attention are connected with the existence and the worsening of regional 'inequalities'.

The main proposition I shall maintain is that regional inequalities affected the modality and the intensity of the utilization of the labour force, and, therefore, the direction and the intensity of technical progress during the different phases of the process of Italian development. In particular they might be the cause of a substantial stability of total employment over the long run, and therefore of the drastic lowering of the population's activity rate.

According to my hypothesis the existence and growth of regional inequalities made the Italian economic system more flexible in terms of labour supply than it would have been in a better-balanced regional situation, given an equal rate of employment in the various sectors of the economy; or, in other words, that it gave the Italian economic system the possibility of a higher rate of technical progress for a given investment rate, than would have occurred in a well-balanced regional situation. The depressed regions (from now on I shall call them 'southern regions' in a wide sense) have allowed the retention of flexibility in the labour market for whatever type of labour is demanded by firms (in terms, that is, of the characteristics more frequently requested from workers).

These theses are intended to disprove the most common interpretative hypotheses on 'dualism', as well as those which refer to Southern regions as the 'home colonies' of Italy. In particular, I intend to disprove two specific aspects of these theses. According to the first one, the Italian system is characterized by modern (capitalist) activities mainly concentrated in the Northern regions, and by backward (precapitalist) activities concentrated in the southern regions. The permanence of underdeveloped areas (both sectors and regions) is caused by the fact that for a number of historical reasons the capitalist relations of production have not yet been able to encompass the whole economy. According to the second aspect of these theses, the Southern areas have been exploited by Northern regions in a kind of 'colonial' relationship. I am suggesting, on the contrary, that the modes of production both in developed and in backward areas are capitalist (the possible permanence of precapitalist forms being a function of the development of the most advanced part of the economy) and that the relationships (certainly of exploitation) between Northern areas and Southern areas cannot be called 'colonial' without the use of this term being allowed to generate more confusion than clarity in the debate.

Regional inequalities in a historical perspective

The difference in the level of per capita income between the various Italian regions has shown a marked tendency to increase both in the long term and in much of the more limited period from the postwar years until the present. It is probable that these differences grew more noticeably in periods when the rate of growth of the whole economy was higher and in particular during the first part of each of the different periods that I shall call 'Giolitti's' (1897–1913), 'Fascist' (1922–1938), and 'Republican' (1951–1970).

In figure 1 some indicators of regional inequality in Italy over the long term are compared. Indicators 1 and 2 were constructed by Williamson (1965). The first one measures regional inequalities in terms of net per capita output (1938 lire) and is based on SVIMEZ (1954) data for the prewar years and on Tagliacarne series for the postwar years; the second indicator measures the same inequalities in terms of the ratio between employment in agriculture and total number of employed, and is based on

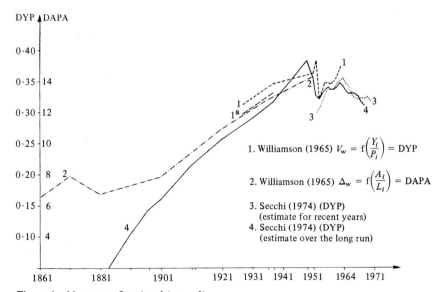

1. Williamson (1965) $V_w = f\left(\dfrac{Y_i}{P_i}\right) = $ DYP

2. Williamson (1965) $\Delta_w = f\left(\dfrac{A_i}{L_i}\right) = $ DAPA

3. Secchi (1974) (DYP)
   (estimate for recent years)
4. Secchi (1974) (DYP)
   (estimate over the long run)

Figure 1. Measures of regional inequality.

census data. The third indicator measures the differences in terms of net
per capita income (1963 lire) and is derived from ISTAT (1974) data (my
elaboration); the fourth indicator is derived by extending to the period
between 1881 and 1951 some relationships, verified for the period 1952–
1969, between the inequalities expressed in terms of net per capita
income and some variables of which it is possible to build the long-period
series [such as GDP (gross domestic product), GDP rate of growth, rate of
increase in internal migration, and changes in the structure of regional
employment and in the sectoral composition of national output]. Hence
the third indicator supplies us with a reliable 'measure' (within the limits
of reliability of official statistics) of the regional differences in the years
after 1951 (average triennial values are used in figure 1, so that the series
begins in 1952), whereas the fourth indicator represents an 'estimate' of
the levels and of the trends of the differences during the period between
1881 and 1951 [1].

The only conclusion that can be reached, on the basis of the various
calculations, is that the difference in level of per capita income in the
different regions is much higher today than in 1951 and 1881; it grew
remarkably even during the most intense periods of development of the
Italian economic system, and perhaps more in 'Giolitti's' and the
'Republican' periods than in any other. As for the period in the immediate
past, the differences were probably at a peak between 1949 and 1962
(this last date seems to me more reliable). Yet these dates could prove in
the future to have been only *relative* maxima.

This process of increasing inequality has been interpreted in a number
of ways, but few of them are susceptible to systematic empirical verification.
However, in these interpretations, most attention has been paid to the
problem of the initial occurrence of differences among the regions; with
this explained, it is accepted that mechanisms of a cumulative type act.
But this is not quite satisfactory. It is most probable that in the secular
development of our economic system (excluding the 'war' periods) there

[1] In Secchi (1974) I illustrate the methods used to build the fourth indicator, and
the reasons why I think that the trend during the periods between the wars may be
considered as sufficiently reliable. In these limited periods the trends of the various
indicators are rather similar. The same cannot be said of the levels of the only
comparable indicators 1 and 4; however, it is necessary to bear in mind that in his
estimates Williamson uses a 'regional' disaggregation (nineteen regions) of the national
territory, whereas my indicators are built by using a 'divisional' disaggregation (four
divisions); moreover, the level of the indicator of differences used by both Williamson
and myself depends on the size of the territorial disaggregation. Thus, Williamson's
first indicator when recalculated on a divisional basis (curve 1[a] in figure 1) is very
close, even in terms of level, to my last indicator. The difference which still exists
can perhaps be explained by the fact that, as Williamson has recourse to the SVIMEZ
series, he measures the differences among the regions in terms of net per capita output
in the private sector, whereas my indicator estimates the differences in terms of net
per capita total income.

has been on the one hand a number of phases in which an 'intensive' use of the labour force prevailed and, on the other hand, phases in which the labour force was used 'extensively'. The former phases present a higher demand for labour (especially in the labour-intensive sectors), the latter obviously have the opposite characteristics.

During the phases in which the labour force is used extensively, important flows of labour take place between the various productive sectors; to them corresponds a marked tendency to regional specialization, that is, high rates of increase in the index of regional labour concentration (CN, see figures 2 and 3). This, of course, gives rise to even more remarkable migration flows towards the urban areas. In these periods, the inequality increases because the sectors which express a high demand for labour (and the development of which is strongly export-led in a direct or indirect way) are located in the North, and because the development process in these phases is marked in the same (industrial) sectors by strong (internal and external) scale economies. In these sectors the productivity of labour is likely to grow at a higher rate than wages. Moreover, it grows more than in other sectors where scale economies do not exist and where the rates of increase of labour productivity and wages are very similar.

Hence, in these phases, the intersectoral variation in labour productivity increases more than that in wages (which will be increasing generally), and

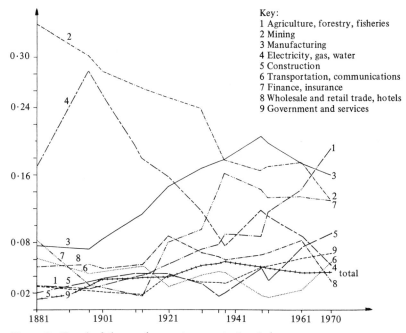

Figure 2. Trend of the employment concentration index.

the rate of increase of labour productivity (high) is greater than that of wages (low). In many sectors, in fact, the rate of increase of labour productivity tends to be correlated with the rate of increase of output and of the index of the regional concentration of the labour force (CN, see figures 2 and 3). The existence of a relationship between the rate of increase of labour productivity and the rate of increase of output (which constitutes Verdoorn's law) is usually assumed to be merely an indicator of economies of scale. In the same way, the existence of a relationship with the rate of increase in the index of the regional concentration of labour might be interpreted as corroborating the indications of the existence of scale economies, when the correlation is positive, and of scale diseconomies, where the same correlation is negative.

In fact, however, during the phases in which the labour force is used intensively, the movements towards the urban areas, and the migration flows (to which correspond still relatively moderate intersectoral labour flows) are lower than those of the preceding (extensive) phases. The workers employed during these phases show a spatial concentration similar to that of the population, so that the indices of regional labour concentration are rather stable or decreasing. In these periods the regional inequality increases less than in the preceding phases.

During the phases of intensive utilization of the labour force, the demand for labour has a prevailingly 'selective' character: 'weak' workers

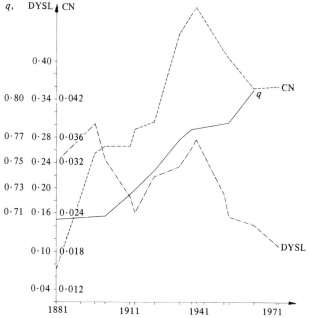

Figure 3. Urban concentration (q), regional concentration of employment (CN), and intersectoral variability of labour productivity (DYSL).

Table 1. Measures of regional inequality: levels.

	1881	1897	1913	1921	1938	1949	1952	1958	1963	1965	1970
DPP[a]	0·0097	0·0549	0·0935	0·1269	0·1708	0·1899	0·1630	0·1687	0·1740	0·1631	0·1490
DPL	0·0232	0·0311	0·0280	0·0530	0·0758	0·0931	0·0737	0·0757	0·0595	0·0559	0·0572
DAP	0·0288	0·0716	0·0827	0·0869	0·1203	0·1074	0·0951	0·1286	0·1188	0·1148	0·1033
DAPA	0·0829	0·0883	0·0619	0·0758	0·1658	0·1418	0·2133	0·1950	0·2726	0·2693	0·3607
DAPI	0·1496	0·1840	0·2904	0·3263	0·4158	0·4003	0·4074	0·3619	0·3497	0·3224	0·3112
DAPIM	0·1654	0·2152	0·3369	0·4030	0·4961	0·5682	0·4588	0·4881	0·5027	0·4715	0·4620
DYP	0·0069	0·1431	0·2225	0·2560	0·3158	0·3809	0·2960	0·3372	0·3370	0·3210	0·3156

[a] Terms are defined in the appendix.

Table 2. Measures of regional inequality: average annual rates of increase.

	1881–1897	1897–1913	1913–1921	1921–1938	1938–1949	1952–1958	1958–1963	1963–1965	1965–1970
DPP[a]	8·75	3·25	3·79	1·73	0·96	0·57	0·62	-3·23	-1·81
DPL	1·82	-0·66	7·72	2·08	1·86	0·45	-4·79	-3·12	0·46
DAP	5·33	0·90	0·62	1·90	-1·03	4·99	-1·58	-1·71	-2·11
DAPA	0·39	-2·20	2·52	4·38	-1·42	-1·49	6·64	-0·61	5·80
DAPI	1·29	2·80	1·45	1·20	-0·35	-1·97	-0·69	-4·06	-0·71
DAPIM	1·64	2·76	2·23	1·22	1·23	1·03	0·59	-3·20	-0·41
DYP	20·86	2·80	1·77	1·24	1·72	2·20	-0·01	-2·40	-0·34
Ẏ	0·67	2·70	0·70	2·20	1·10	4·97	5·82	3·89	5·33

[a] Terms are defined in the appendix.

are expelled from the labour market, 'strong' workers remain in it or enter it. The reasons why a worker is included in one group or in the other obviously vary with the productive technique in each phase. This means that these phases are probably characterized (in spite of aggregate rates of growth which are generally lower than the rates characteristic of extensive phases) by a high rate of increase of labour productivity, by a decrease in intersectoral variation in labour productivity, by a rate of increase of (industrial) wages higher than in preceding phases, and by a decrease in the intersectoral variation in wages.

Unfortunately, the lack of data (in particular, the lack of a historical series on employed workers which is not limited to a few points in time) does not allow verification of all of these propositions. However, the

Table 3. Principal features of the 'extensive' and 'intensive' phases (average annual rates of increase calculated on average triennial values).

Year	$\dot{Y}$	$\dot{E}$	$\dot{D}YP$	$\dot{w}$	$\dot{s}$	$\dot{E}s$
Extensive phase						
1897–1906	2·86	9·49	3·07	1·60	1·97	4·64
1921–1928	2·98	7·30	1·62	−0·02	0·38	4·89
1952–1963	5·24	4·83	1·18	6·03	6·82	11·55
Intensive phase						
1906–1913	2·70	−1·55	1·45	4·16	1·27	1·41
1928–1938	1·92	3·82	1·35	−1·89	1·41	−3·78
1963–1969	5·08	−3·00	−0·59	9·39[a]	3·63[a]	11·47

[a] 1963–1966.

Key:
$\dot{Y}$ is average annual rate of increase of gross domestic output
$\dot{E}$ is average annual rate of increase of internal migrations
$\dot{w}$ is average annual rate of increase of real (industrial) wages
$\dot{s}$ is average annual rate of increase of real (public administration) wages
$\dot{E}s$ is average annual rate of increase of exports

Table 4. Measures of regional inequality (triennial averages).

	1952	1958	1963	1965	1969
DY_nP	0·2960	0·3372	0·3370	0·3210	0·3233
DCIP	0·2410	0·2476	0·2046	0·1905	0·1762
DCP	0·2264	0·2209	0·1901	0·1860	0·1757
DIP	0·3290	0·3290	0·2660	0·2280	0·1935
$DC_{pr}P$	0·2450	0·2426	0·2120	0·2078	0·1971
DYL_p	0·1382	0·1493	0·1538	0·1480	0·1615
DLP	0·0951	0·1286	0·1188	0·1148	0·1072
DL_pP	0·1466	0·1706	0·1515	0·1437	0·1331
DAP	–	–	0·1029	0·1052	0·0904

phases of 'extensive' development appear to be approximately the following periods: 1897–1906, 1922–1928, 1952–1963; and the 'intensive' phases, the periods 1906–1913, 1928–1938, 1963–1970. Details of the trends in regional inequalities are given in tables 1–4.

Regional inequalities: 1951–1970
The period between 1952 and 1970 can be more precisely divided into four phases: the first one (1952–1958) seems to have the characteristics of the phases here called 'extensive'; that is, when an extensive utilization of the labour force prevails. The last part of the period (1965–1970) seems on the contrary to be an 'intensive' phase. The two middle phases represent the period (1958–1963), during which the strategy of extensive development begins to show deep internal contradictions, and the period (1963–1965) in which these contradictions help to produce the crisis of the whole economic system showing the necessity of a new (intensive) development strategy.

In the very first period (1952–1958), the regional differences in terms of net per capita income grew considerably, the aggregate rate of increase of employment was positive, the index of regional concentration of employment was growing, as was the intersectoral variation in real wages (in industry), and internal migration flows increased significantly, as did investment in urban areas and housing.

During the last of the four periods (1965–1970), on the contrary, the regional differences were still increasing (even if modestly), there was a decrease in employment, the index of regional concentration of employment was decreasing or stationary, the intersectoral variation in labour

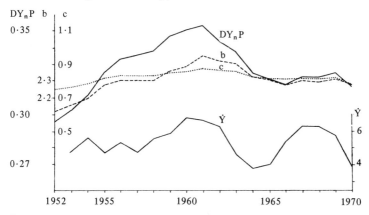

Figure 4. Measures of regional differences: DY_nP is net per capita income at market prices (1963 lire); b is the same inequality with the formula: $b = Y_{NW}/Y_S$, where Y_{NW} is net per capita income in North West Italy, Y_S is net per capita income in Southern Italy, $\overline{Y}$ is national average; c is the same inequality with the formula: $c = (Y_{NW} - Y_S)/\overline{Y}$; $\dot{Y}$ is the rate of growth of GDP at factor cost (1963 lire, moving triennial averages).

productivity was decreasing and so was the intersectoral variation in wages; migration flows and housing investment increased less than during the former phases. These trends also seem to coincide with those in the long (secular) period.

During the latest 'extensive' phase (1952–1958), differentials still increased in terms of net per capita income, per capita investments, labour productivity, and the rate of total and permanent employment. This meant that income and output, productive capacity, and employment were regionally concentrated (relative to the population, which nevertheless grew differently in the various regions as a result of strong migration flows). The productive sectors mainly responsible for the concentration of income, production, and employment in the Northern regions were the industrial ones: perhaps the major firms belonging to the 'basic' industrial sectors (such as heavy chemicals, oil refining, paper mills) were dominant in terms of output, whereas the small firms belonging to backward sectors and to the building sector were dominant in terms of employment. To the increasing regional concentration of employment and population corresponded, of course, strong interregional migration flows and a marked outflow of labour from the agricultural sector. These flows seemed to find their principal origin among the independent workers[2] in the South and caused a noticeable decrease in marginal workers, chiefly in the South. If one considers only the outflow of labour from agriculture, the extensive phase was characterized by an initial outflow of dependent and independent workers as well as by a continuous decrease in marginal and permanent workers in all regions. This also corresponded to a considerable decline in the activity rate (a trend which was stronger in the backward regions).

During the 'intensive' phase, all the indicators of regional inequality (with the exception of those of permanent labour productivity and net per capita income) had a decreasing or a substantially stationary trend. This means that productive capacity and employment did not concentrate regionally relative to the population (which continued to concentrate in the North Western regions because of different regional rates of demographic increase due to migration movements). In this period the 'basic' industrial sectors located new productive capacity in a more

[2] The categories of workers referred to follow the definitions used by the Italian National Institute of Statistics (ISTAT), and fall into two groups, independent and dependent workers being defined together, and marginal and permanent. *Independent workers* are employers and independent professionals, 'autonomous' workers (craftsmen, farmers, dealers, etc) and their relatives working with them. *Dependent workers* are manual and nonmanual employees, salaried staff and managers. *Marginal workers* are underemployed (with not more than thirty-two hours worked a week, excepting teachers), casual workers, and workers in any other form of precarious employment (both dependent and independent). *Permanent workers* are all other (than marginal) workers (both dependent and independent).

geographically uniform pattern (it is these sectors, and especially steel and petrochemicals, which were mainly responsible for the decrease in the differences in terms of investment per inhabitant). The employment in the other industrial sectors concentrated in the North West inside the 'modern' sectors, and in the South in the 'backward' ones. The building sector reduced its own demand for labour in the North West and increased it in the South. Employment in public administration increased more and more in the Southern regions.

At the national level, employment decreased: this corresponded to a decline in independent and marginal workers. Conversely, the labour outflow from agriculture concerned both dependent and independent workers (but mostly the latter), both permanent and marginal workers (and mostly the former). At the same time there was a further increase in the ratio of dependent workers to the whole body of workers (although this did not concern all regions to the same extent: it was notable in North West and Central Italy), and with a smaller increase in the ratio of permanent workers to the total (this ratio, however, was already about 90%). This process corresponded, finally, to a drastic lowering of the activity rate. The decline at first concerned only women, mainly in backward regions, but then took in both sexes (mainly males in developed regions and females in backward regions).

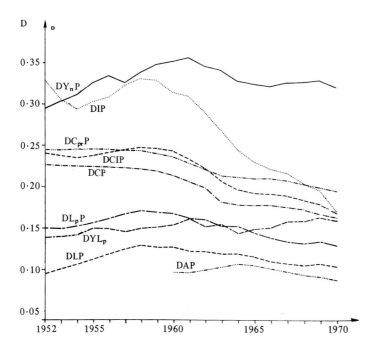

Figure 5. Trend of the regional differences.

During the two middle phases, the regional inequality (in terms of per capita income) was decreasing; employment was also decreasing, at first (1958–1963) in all the regions except the North West, then (1963–1965) in the North West more than in the other regions; at first only among the independent workers in all the regions (which meant that in the first of the two middle phases dependent workers in the North West were increasing), then among the dependent and independent workers in all the regions (and in the North West chiefly among the dependent workers); at first only among the marginal workers in all regions and then among the marginal and permanent workers (and in all regions, except the South, chiefly among the permanent ones).

As for the sectors, the decrease in employment during the first of the middle phases (1958–1963) concerned exclusively and in all regions the backward sectors and, of course, agriculture. During the second of the middle phases (1963–1965) the decrease was in the advanced industrial sectors (not the backward ones), the building sector and, of course, agriculture. Thus during the first of the middle phases the decrease in employment concerned mainly the independent workers (in backward and agricultural sectors), whereas during the second it concerned chiefly the dependent workers (in advanced industrial sectors and in building) and the permanent workers (in both industrial and agricultural sectors).

This pattern suggests a hypothesis according to which the first of these phases would be characterized by intense intersectoral and interregional mobility of labour, and the second by an expulsion of workers (chiefly females, since the female activity rate during this period was strongly decreasing) from the labour market. In all probability a strong intersectoral mobility of labour took place only during the 1958–1963 period: from backward regions to highly developed regions, from backward sectors to the advanced ones. During the other phases the flows in and out of the labour market as a whole were dominant (except for the building industry in the extensive phase).

During the 1958–1963 phase, the rate of aggregate development was quite high; and so was the rate of increase in labour productivity, both in advanced industrial sectors and, above all, in the backward ones (as opposed to the pattern in the extensive phase) and in agriculture. The rate of increase in labour productivity would be still higher had a large share of employment not been absorbed by the building sector. The contribution of the intersectoral movements of labour to the rate of increase of labour productivity in the advanced industrial sectors was also considerable (at least significantly higher than in the other phases).

The development of the advanced industrial sectors, increasingly concentrated in the North West, and of agriculture in the South, took place in this phase by 'drawing out' labour from backward sectors and regions, but of course not all the workers who left these regions and sectors found employment in the advanced regions and sectors.

The opposite happened during the second of the middle phases: the crisis of the advanced sectors and of the building sector began with an expulsion of workers from these sectors (which kept up the rate of increase of labour productivity); some of them entered the backward sectors (where employment was increasing). It is very likely that the 'quality' of the workers who now entered the backward sectors was different from (and lower than) that of the workers who quit them in the preceding phase: in fact, the intersectoral movements of labour contributed negatively to the rate of increase in labour productivity in the backward sectors during both phases. We may suppose that in the 1958–1963 period young male and skilled workers left these sectors, responding to the demand for labour expressed by the advanced industrial sectors. On the other hand, during the 1963–1965 period, workers with the opposite characteristics entered the backward sectors, either because they were driven out from the same advanced industrial sectors, or because they were leaving agriculture and were unable to find employment in the building industry, as they could have done in the preceding phases. This is probably the reason why in the 1963–1965 period other workers delayed their own departure from the agricultural sector (the rate of increase of agricultural employment was still negative, but lower in absolute terms than that of the immediately preceding and subsequent phases). In this phase, finally, the interregional movements of labour contributed negatively to the rate of increase of labour productivity (both in the North West and in the South).

Regional inequalities and the accumulation strategies (or development)
My thesis is that the different phases correspond to different development strategies pursued by the various leading economic sectors and social groups.

As I pointed out, the 'extensive' phases are characterized by a type of development in which the capital:labour ratio grows moderately and, hence, total employment increased. The 'intensive' phases, on the contrary, are typified by a higher rate of increase in the capital:labour ratio and, usually, by a decrease in employment. These features derive both from the sectoral composition of the gross product increase and from the type of production techniques used by each sector. These two factors are themselves the result, as far as the result can be measured, of the development strategy characterizing each phase: that is to say of the alliances among the different social groups and of the production choices made by each of them.

The resemblances between the various 'extensive' and 'intensive' phases, as well as the differences, are not limited to the trend of regional disparities and the demand for labour. The 'extensive' phases are always characterized by higher rates of aggregate growth, internal migration, export, and regional concentration of employment; by lower rates of increase of industrial wages; by an increasing intersectoral variability of wages, by a higher urbanization of the population, and by higher rates of investment in housing. The accumulation process is supported, during the 'extensive' phases, by a rate of increase of wages which is lower than that of labour productivity, and by the expropriation of an increasing proportion of the worker's current income (during the latest phase, this occurred through a relative rise in the price of housing brought about by the building and real-estate sector). During the 'intensive' phases, on the contrary, accumulation is supported by a higher rate of exploitation of the employed labour force (through an intensification of the labour process) and of the working class as a whole (through a worsening of the 'urban condition'). The 'extensive' phases also correspond, usually, to 'intercapitalist' alliances which are wider than those of the 'intensive' phases.

As to the formation and growth of regional inequalities, the 'extensive' phases correspond to a strong concentration of production and employment in the developed areas; in the backward regions the 'intensive' phases to a process of disindustrialization (to the ruin of small independent producers and of small firms outside the expanding sectors), and to an increasing concentration of firms into an oligopolistic structure.

The shift from one phase to another during the postwar period seems to have sprung from the development of major contradictions specific to each pattern of development. This is true in particular for the shift from extensive phases to intensive phases. Some of these contradictions are specifically related to problems of a territorial nature, and their understanding becomes particularly important in the interpretation of the two 'crises' of the Italian economic system during the same period.

In my hypothesis, the 1964 crisis had an important cause in an 'excessive' development of the building sector; this, in its turn, had its own origins, chiefly in the spatial concentration of the labour force and of the population in the preceding years. Finally, this concentration was itself due in large measure to the main features of the industrial strategy of the 1950s. The 1970 crisis, on the other hand, was a result largely of the effects of the 'urban' situation (in a wide sense) on the cost of reproduction of the labour force, itself once again a result in large measure of the industrial strategy of the 1960s.

The first crisis appeared mainly as a conflict between the 'advanced' industrial sectors and the building industry; the second one appeared as a more generalized conflict among some 'advanced' sectors, between 'advanced' and backward sectors, between capital and labour, and among some groups of workers.

The first crisis was faced by the proposal of 'reforms' (with a strong territorial content), implying above all the explosion of a sharp intra-capitalist conflict over the proposals for the planned control of urban development. Such proposals were designed to transfer resources towards those social groups most affected by the increase in rents linked to the boom in the building industry. The second crisis could not be overcome in this way because of the difficulty, perhaps the impossibility, of achieving 'reforms' (still with a strong territorial content), other than those already implemented, to eliminate some of the distortions produced in the past. Such distortions included backwardness in agriculture, inefficiencies in the public sector, structural imbalances between supply and demand in the housing market, urban crisis, structural and regional imbalances in the labour market, and strong interregional migration movements. Their effects consisted, in the first instance, of the increased cost of reproduction of the labour force.

The analysis of some territorial aspects of Italian economic development should therefore reveal certain difficulties specific to the different development strategies, and should also indicate some of the reasons why these strategies were chosen, modified, and forsaken. In other words, it is probable that an analysis of territorial aspects of Italian economic development could clarify some of the principal alliances and conflicts among the different groups and classes on which this development has been based in different periods. It should not, of course, be forgotten that the development and the crisis of the Italian economic system also have explanations other than those we have just considered. There should be no misunderstanding about this. It is not intended to ascribe to the aspects presented here a significance beyond their contribution. But it is important to avoid wide, general, and often unsatisfactory analysis and to try to move at a more limited, but more detailed, level. This is why I believe it to be necessary to attempt to specify the nature of certain inequalities and problems which emerged during the growth and the crisis of the Italian economic system: those of a territorial nature. It is also important to clarify the nature of the alliances and conflicts which are characteristic of these years, and which are connected with the same problems, and to try to isolate the various groups acting in these periods and to analyze the objective bases of their behaviour. The fact that other aspects of Italian economic development are here neglected does not mean they are unimportant (even from a territorial point of view).

Conclusions

What has been said should adequately justify my initial statements. In particular, it should explain why I do not consider as acceptable the 'dualistic' hypotheses and these which refer to the Southern regions as 'home colonies'. It should also explain why I think the Italian example could perhaps be adopted to some other countries, perhaps during particular phases of their economic development.

I believe the Italian example may be characteristic of countries without important raw materials, in which a modern sector (technically advanced) with a labour force representing a sufficiently modest part of the total employed labour force (for example less than a quarter) coexists with backward sectors employing, in contrast, a very large part of the labour force, and where the excess of supply over demand for any type of labour is large (that is, overpopulated countries). All three conditions seem to me to be important.

These countries represent, perhaps, a group different from others where a modern sector also coexists, or used to coexist, with a backward one, but where there is neither a great lack of raw materials nor a surplus population, and where, nonetheless, regional inequalities may be, or may have been, quite considerable.

A close examination of the history of some countries belonging to the last group, in particular the United States and Canada, has led some scholars to affirm that regional inequalities are typical of the 'first phases' of the economic development of a country. These inequalities tend to increase until the country reaches a certain level of development, and then to decrease successively, as happened in the USA and Canada (Williamson, 1965).

My opinion is that in the countries belonging to the first group, among which is Italy, the process will be different from that in the USA and Canada. In these countries economic development may not be achieved unless regional inequalities are retained, and possibly increased. This means, of course, that, in given historical conditions, in these countries no other system of intercapitalist alliances (national or international) can be formed, than those implying economic policies consistent with increasing regional imbalance. This is at least what the past seems to tell us.

References

ISTAT, 1974 *Annuario di Contabilita Nazionale,* Italian National Institute of Statistics, Rome

Secchi B, 1974 *Squilibri Regionali e Sviluppo Economico*, Marsilio, Padova

SVIMEZ, 1954 *Statistiche sul Mezzogiorno: 1861-1953,* Rome

Williamson J G, 1965 "Regional inequality and the process of national development: a description of the pattern" in *Economic Development and Cultural Change* 13 3-84

Appendix

The indicators of regional inequality for which an attempt was made to estimate the trend and the terms in which they were measured are the following:

DYP   is net per capita income at market prices.
DPP   is gross domestic per capita product (at factor prices).
DPL   is gross domestic product per worker (at factor prices).
DAP   is activity rate.
DAPA   is activity rate in agriculture.
DAPI   is activity rate in industry.
DAPIM   is activity rate in manufacturing.
DY_nP is net per capita income (at market prices), 1963 lire.
DCIP   is per capita consumption plus investment, 1963 lire.
DCP   is per capita consumption, 1963 lire.
$DC_{pr}P$ is per capita private consumption, 1963 lire.
DIP   is per capita investment, 1963 lire.
DYL_p is gross product (at factor prices), per permanent worker, 1963 lire.
DLP   is total number of employed.
DL_pP is permanent number of employed.

The type of indicator used, in each case, is the one proposed by Williamson (1965):

$$V_w = \frac{\left\{ \sum_i [y_i - \bar{y}]^2 p_i/P \right\}^{\frac{1}{2}}}{\bar{y}} \qquad (i = 1, 2, 3, 4) \, .$$

Hence for example

$$DYP = \frac{\left\{ \sum_i [(YP_i) - (\overline{YP})]^2 p_i/P \right\}^{\frac{1}{2}}}{\overline{YP}} \qquad (i = 1, 2, 3, 4) \, .$$

In each case a four-region territorial disaggregation (that is, into 'divisions') has been used: North West Italy, North East Italy, Central Italy, and Southern Italy. The four divisions are the ones commonly used by ISTAT for territorial economic accounting.

As for the monetary indicators of differences, series were presented at constant prices: at 1938 prices until 1952, at 1963 prices since 1952 (in the figures and in the tables the year 1952 appears at 1963 prices; the rate of increase between 1949 and 1952 is calculated by using 1952 values at 1938 prices). When possible, average triennial values were used for the calculation of the indicators.

The deviations of the regional values from the national average were weighted by the percentage share of the regional population over the whole population in all the indicators of which the third letter is a P (for example: DYP, DAPIM, etc) and with the percentage share of workers in the indicators in which the third letter is an L (DPL).

Coal Combines and Interregional Uneven Development in the UK

J CARNEY
Regional Policy Research Unit, Durham
J LEWIS
Cambridge University
R HUDSON
Regional Policy Research Unit, Durham

Introduction

The explanation of the emergence and persistence of a 'regional problem' in the UK during this century is important both in the construction of a theory of late capitalism (Mandel, 1975, pages 89–90) and in understanding the long-term decline of British capitalism. In this paper we put forward part of our contribution to such an explanation by exploring the relationships between coal combines and interregional uneven development.

The position in 1914: combine structure and coalfield conditions

Coal combines were monopolistic amalgamations of interests which originated in the appropriation of surplus value produced in the coalfields. Something of their character in 1914 is evident in the *Stock Exchange Official Intelligence and Yearbook* for that year. The following illustration from the Northeast typifies the interrelated nature of coal mining, branches of production, and other activities such as transport and banking that had become established on *all* the major UK coalfields by 1914 (see Heinemann, 1944).

The branches of production and of other activities listed below, all well represented in terms of fixed capital and size of employed labour force, were to be found in the Northeast in the period 1900 to 1914. This was a boom period for the listed branches of activity, although the boom was expressed in dividend payments and not in an upsurge of new investment in constant or variable capital. All the branches of activity listed below were closely and intricately connected through directorships, shareholdings, loans, debentures, rents (mineral and wayleave royalties), transfer pricing, quota and output arrangements, trade and employer association membership, and political alignment against the rising Labour Party. The branches of activity were:

(a) coal, iron and steel, and shipbuilding;
(b) gas;
(c) electricity (both production and transmission);
(d) water;
(e) insurance companies and banks;
(f) railways (freight and passenger), tramways, coastal and ocean shipping;

(g) wholesaling and retailing (relating to commodities used in production or for capitalist or working-class consumption);

(h) housing trusts for the provision of housing for the working class;

(i) investment trusts for investment in land, minerals, and currency; or loan speculation;

(j) electrical engineering, chemicals, and other 'new' production-goods industries.

In addition, the companies which formed combines within the Northeast and at the time had most of their assets fixed in that region had strong interregional links with combines based on other coalfields. These links were in terms of ownership (although, at the time, penetration of capital originating in one major coalfield into another in the form of ordinary shareholdings on a substantial scale was absent), 'overlapping' directorships (of which there were very many and which were developed into an intricate network), pricing and quota agreements (which were not at all stable at that time), debenture guarantees and other credit arrangements, lobbying in defence of combine interests, wage fixing, and labour control policies.

The major companies on the other coalfields in the UK were similar to those in the Northeast in that they embraced varied branches of production and other activities. These companies were:

(1) Powell Duffryn (South Wales),

(2) Stavely Sheepbridge (Yorkshire, Derbyshire, Nottinghamshire),

(3) Bolsover Colliery (Derbyshire, Nottinghamshire),

(4) Amalgamated Anthracite Collieries Ltd. (South Wales),

(5) Partridge, Jones and John Paton (South Wales),

(6) Coltness Iron-Wilson's and Clyde (Lanarkshire, Fife, West Lothian),

(7) William Baird and Co. Ltd. (Dumfries),

(8) Manchester Collieries Ltd. (Lancashire),

(9) Carlton Main Colliery Co. Ltd. (Yorkshire),

(10) Ocean Coal and Wilsons (South Wales),

(11) United Steel Co. (Yorkshire, Cumberland),

(12) Fife Coal Co. (Fife, Kinross),

(13) B A Collieries (Nottinghamshire),

(14) Stanton Ironworks Ltd. (Stewarts and Lloyds) (Nottinghamshire),

(15) Edinburgh–Lothian Group (Midlothian, East Lothian),

(16) Henry Briggs and Co. Ltd. (Yorkshire).

As well as dense interconnections between interests within coalfields and between coalfields—so that George Harvey (1917) could correctly remark that "capital knows no county"—there had been a considerable *direct* internationalisation of capital originating from the coalfields of the UK. Usually this was to ensure supplies of essential raw materials or to open up new markets for output (as in the case of Bell Brothers of Teesside who dominated the Latin American rail-network construction). Sometimes surplus value was used so as to promote the formation of international cartels (as in the case of the nickel users' cartel). In addition to this form of investment overseas, the capital originating in the coalfields was used to sustain *portfolio* investment (especially in the political Empire of the UK but also in Latin America). This investment was mainly in the form of interest-bearing capital lent to the State in the receiving society or to companies interested in provision of infrastructure essential to the further penetration of capital into such societies.

By 1914 in each coalfield the end result of this form of investment of realised surplus value, coupled with the use of surplus value to restrict entry, to effect amalgamations, and to sustain lavish capitalist consumption (all of which were not directly aimed at increasing the fixed capital of the coalfields), was a restriction in the advance of the productive forces in the various branches of activity which made up the combines. An indication of this was the slow pace of introduction of the 'latest' (often American and German) advances in methods of production, especially of electrification and mechanisation in the coal mines. In turn this affected costs of production, output productivity, and competitiveness of combine output in the world market. Information produced by the Sankey Committee in 1919 indicated that the high proportion of old mines compared to foreign coalfields, combined with high proportions of coal cut by hand and transported by animals, and low wages, could be related to low levels of investment in the years prior to their report. From the Northeast, there is also some evidence that there was an increase in amalgamation and cartel tendencies in the branches of production dominated by the combines. This was accompanied by tendencies to deliberate restriction of output to drive up prices. The result of this was widespread below-capacity working, not only in the coal companies but also in iron- and steelmaking and shipbuilding. The wartime governments did not do much to restrict such strategies for maintaining the rate of profit.

In the coalfields this level of capacity working had both short- and long-period consequences for population distribution. In the short-period it implied a large relative surplus population, which affected conditions of consumption and thus the reproduction of labour power—directly for those rendered surplus and indirectly for those still employed, since the bargaining strength of the combine owners was increased. The long-period changes in demand for labour power which arose from alterations in the rate of profit, the prevailing technology, and control of the labour process, affected the rate of migration between the coalfields and the rest of the space economy. It was the coincidence of a short-period fluctuation in the level of capacity working with the long-period stagnation in the interwar years that was immediately expressed in severe overcrowding in working-class housing, high levels of child mortality, and dietary deficiencies (see data collected by Mess, 1928).

Another aspect of the situation in the coalfields around 1914 relates to the social relationships underlying the rate and mass of resource exploitation under the combines. A brief interpretation is as follows. In the short-period, the rate of resource exploitation and the mass of resources removed[1] in given technical conditions of production were contingent upon the level of capacity working, itself related to the rate of capital accumulation and shares of production in the world market. Resource exploitation was also related to the age of fixed capital stock and to geological conditions. In the long-period, resources were defined by changes in the technical conditions of production, as these affected the amounts and types of raw materials used to produce other commodities. Effective demand for different kinds of coal or ironstone, for instance, varied considerably over the long-period. Moreover the rate of introduction of new fixed capital, resulting from decisions on the disposal of realised surplus value, determined the pace of technological changes in production. This in turn altered effective demand and also altered the set of resources and locations embraced by that effective demand for the raw materials of production.

If the pace of capital accumulation in the combines was linked to resource definition and exploitation, conversely, restrictions in output and hence restrictions on the realisation of surplus value and on new investment in fixed capital in activities winning coal or ironstone, for example, often created situations where resources were defined out of existence. It became 'cheaper' for combines to write off collieries and allow flooding and consequent destruction of reserves rather than to reinvest a portion of realised surplus value in the surface and below-ground fixed capital necessary to turn the reserves into use values[2]. In the Northeast the case of Southwest Durham in the interwar period repeated the experience of the Tyneside collieries in the 1830s, the pits were allowed to flood and reserves were destroyed in this manner on a mass scale.

The interwar period: combines and crises
In the Northeast and in many other coalfields low rates of fixed-capital formation had become the dominant feature of the combine operations before 1914. The tendency became both marked and self-reinforcing in most areas for most of the interwar period, in particular with respect to investment in the means of producing coal. Falling investment in the interwar period was combined with a shrinkage in world markets for combine output and acute competitiveness between national capitalist interests (which were, however, within countries increasingly

[1] Coal, ironstone, fluorspar, limestone, and fireclay were the main raw materials produced in the coalfields under the combines or produced by the combine labour force outside the coalfields but transported there to be consumed.

[2] It is a general principle in a capitalist mode of production that use values are only produced to the extent that they yield exchange values. The behaviour of the combine owners in this case, in writing off collieries and reserves of coal, was *rational* only within the confines of this principle.

monopolistically organised). The UK coal industry and other combine
activities were increasingly uncompetitive in shrinking world markets. In
conditions of overproduction and low levels of capacity working, the
record of low rates of electrification and mechanisation in the coal
industry and in other parts of the combines was now expressed in heavily
falling export sales and declining shares of world markets.

To the capitalists in the combines, searching for 'solutions' to the
unparalleled overproduction crisis, which could not be combatted by
further extensions of or expansion within the Empire, various solutions
seemed to present themselves (see Carney and Hudson, 1975). In the coal
companies the solution to falling shares of export markets was seen by the
owners as involving not an increase in electrification and mechanisation
but rather extension of the working day and wage cuts. The capitalists of
the coal industry were most prominent in the interwar period for the
tenacity with which they followed this policy of wage cutting. Moreover,
these capitalists (who were not separate from the other combine interests)
became successful manipulators of the State apparatus in support of their
policy.

The consequences were expressed not only in the bitter class struggles that
marked the whole of the period in many of the coalfields but also in a
deepening State involvement in the regulation of coal production, of tenure
relations associated with mineral production, and of the coal trade (that is,
quota and price fixing, transfer prices, and so on). The defeats of the
miners in the twenties successfully enforced the coal owners' solution of
wage cutting. This, however, did little to halt the decline in the output of
coal, the fall in UK shares in a declining world market and of course did
nothing to alter the pace of mechanisation or electrification. Wage cutting
did not restore costs of production of coal to a position where the
combines could undercut foreign producers. Other solutions had to be
tried. However, neither the wage cuts nor the State involvement in the
regulation of the mines (and the control of the labouring classes) were
immediately altered. Wage levels were restored to 1923 levels in 1939 in
the Northeast. State involvement continued on an expanding scale.

Other responses to overcapacity occurred. One involved an acceleration
of amalgamations (that is, nonreproductive use of surplus value) *within*
each coalfield and between some companies in the coalfields. These
amalgamations were increasingly prompted by a branch of the State,
namely, the Bank of England. Another response to overcapacity was
simply mass sackings. These occurred in the coalfields after the failure of
wage cutting began to become apparent. Another form of response, which
became prominent in the thirties, was lobbying for protectionism both as
regards tariffs on imports and as regards subsidies to production. (The
setting of import restrictions, although carried out by the State apparatus,
was in effect done in ways 'requested' by the coal and iron and steel
employers' associations.)

A further form of response to the crisis in the interwar period, well exemplified in the case of National Shipbuilders' Securities and the closing of Palmer's Yard at Jarrow in the Northeast, was capacity *reductions* (that is, the physical scrapping of capacity as well as permanent layoffs). Such reductions were thought to be a way of restoring profitability in the shipbuilding industry and were also practised in the coal industry— Cumberland and Southwest Durham are outstanding examples.

An additional response involved 'diversification' out of coal combine branches of activity and into other 'newer' branches of production or into nonproductive branches of activity either in the domestic economy or overseas. In the depressed overseas conditions of the period most attempts at combine diversification were concentrated on banking, insurance, petrol distribution, and electrical engineering; that is, were directed towards strengthening combine involvement already existing in 1914.

Examination of combine structure in 1938 or 1946 (using the *Stock Exchange Yearbook* and the *Colliery Yearbook*) does, however, show that diversification had been limited and that almost precisely the same forms of intraregional, interregional, and international connections as had existed between branches of activity in 1914 were still in existence in 1946. It is important to note that few links existed to the new Department II (means of consumption) industries that became established on a large scale in the Southeast and Midlands during the period. It is also important to note that the new branches of Department I (means of production) industry— oil, mass chemicals, electrical engineering—were closely connected to the old combine structure. The collapse of international portfolio investment in the period of the thirties did not noticeably affect the geographical relations established between capital that had originated in UK coalfields and overseas territories in the period to 1914. There is, however, evidence from Latin America that capital originating from the USA was in the very late thirties in the form of direct investment in raw materials' production, beginning to replace capital originating in the UK.

The interwar period: the establishment of new Department II production
In the terms of orthodox accounts of the interwar period (see Richardson, 1967; Aldcroft and Richardson, 1969) uneven development within the domestic space economy in the UK refers to the dramatic changes in the period 1914 to 1934 in regional unemployment levels. That is, when London and the Southeast are compared with the coalfield areas of 'the North', there was over the period (even though the evidence is not without major defects) a marked reversal of relative positions in terms of levels of male unemployment. In 1914 the Southeast of all the regions in the UK had by far the highest rates of male unemployment, at least double those found in the Northeast and Cumberland and higher than those in Scotland or Northern Ireland. By 1934, although still with a level of male unemployment above 8% as recorded by the

Ministry of Labour, the Southeast, compared to the North, had very little unemployment. This was indicative of the remarkable postwar rise, in that region, of manufacturing production in the 'new' Department II mass consumption goods industries. In effect, this was the first time since the decline of small-scale manufactures in the East End that London and the Southeast could be said to contain productive activity (that is, activity productive of surplus value).

The advance in Department II production in the Southeast contrasted with the stagnation in Department I production in the North (and in shipping and transport dependent on Department I activity). However, the coal combines in the North had generally responded to their overcapacity and profitability crises by wage cutting and mass layoffs (which also affected labour forces engaged in transportation). Consumption was restricted in the working class in the coalfields. This necessitated rudimentary State social control over the relative surplus population to ensure a minimum standard of living so that the surplus population could be reproduced until required in production. In turn, to ensure that public order was preserved amongst the unemployed, it also became necessary for new forms of State social control to be evolved. Early instruments for regulating the poor were found to be inadequate for the purpose of dividing the unemployed from the employed and from each other. New forms of relief were tested out. But, in addition, experimentation in State-initiated labour-transfer and land-settlement schemes was frequently engaged in. Moreover, new forms of ideology, partly arising from the experiments in social control undertaken in certain coalfields, were evolved to legitimate the experimentation, to account for the long depression in ways that would convince or neutralise the working class political and union leadership, and to seek ways out of the depression.

The capitalists most heavily interested in the assets tied up in the depressed coalfields were often active instigators of experiments in trading estates and housing associations, for instance, that were put into operation in the Special Areas. However, some of the State involvement in areas like the Northeast was supported by Lord Nuffield and other Department II capitalists.

There was good reason for the involvement of the Department II capitalists in such activity as was initiated during the late thirties to reconstruct the depressed areas. The crucial restraint on the continued accumulation of capital in the Department II industries of the South was the depressed conditions of consumption in those areas dominated by Department I production. One of the conditions for the success of Department II production in the South was that a large mass of skilled labour was thrown out of work in the North and so acted as a reserve army sustaining reductions in production costs in the South by their presence and sustaining production needs for labour power by their migration south. This mechanism, however, was of subsidiary importance when compared to the massive barrier to further expansion in Department II production that was presented by the great masses of unemployed concentrated in the North.

The limited base for working-class consumption in the coalfields was combined, of course, by this time with an increasingly used up, worn-out stock of fixed capital. Fixed capital depreciation, owing to active use or stagnation and technical obsolescence, involves the transfer of value out of the fixed capital. Clearly, if during booms little realised surplus value is reinvested in replacing value taken out of fixed capital and if, moreover, in slumps, capital stock is depreciating but there is no way of realising surplus value that might be invested in new buildings, plant, and machinery, there is a combination of circumstances that results in mass obsolescence. This is what occurred from 1900 to 1939 in the Northeast and in other older coalfields. Those places where worn-out physical capital stock was concentrated (as was a mass of surplus labour and associated dependents) were bypassed by further advances in the forces of production. Capital equipment and buildings were worn-out in such places. The means of transportation were increasingly falling into disrepair, as was working-class housing. The small stock of capital fixed in health and education facilities for the working class also fell into disrepair and technical obsolescence as compared to more fortunate places.

As a corollary, we should consider why, in circumstances where mass demand for consumption goods was highly restricted in much of the economy, the new consumption-goods industries of the interwar period came to be concentrated in the Southeast. Partly the orthodox explanations about concentrations there of white-collar purchasing power are correct. However, they miss the further issue as to why middle-class strata were reproduced on an expanding scale in this region and also neglect to examine the nature of capitalist consumption in the region. A rather more adequate account of the transformation of the Southeast from 1914 has to deal with the origins of the concentration of mercantile capital in London in the precapitalist trading empire and with the subsequent refinement of the dominance of capitalist interests in activities which appropriate surplus value but do not directly pump it out of the labour they employ. That is, an account of the condition of London in 1914 has to speak of the place of merchant and finance capital in the wide political and imperial empire dominated by capital originating in the UK[3].

[3] The concept of finance capital was first advanced by Hilferding who used it to identify a portion of realised surplus value that was held in money form by various institutions. In our present usage 'finance capital' signifies capital originating and operating as follows: suppose an economy produces more surplus value than can be 'absorbed' as new investment in production in the next production period. The surplus value not reinvested in production constitutes a fund, some or all of which *may* be turned into money capital and thrown into circulation, either domestically or overseas, in order to realise interest. However, the rate of interest is not independent of the rate of profit, nor is the relationship between the two a simple one.

In addition it has to speak of the categories of income which sustained the lavish life styles of the UK bourgeoisie and sustained the speculation and luxury consumer goods production features in conventional accounts.

Even in the unfavourable international financial conditions of the interwar period the revenues from portfolio investment were still sufficient to sustain the advance to mass consumption capitalism 'in one region' in the UK. However, without the reforms begun in the thirties and reaching a climax in the 1945–1951 period there is little to suggest that the interwar transformations worked out in the South could have been sustained over a longer period [4].

It is important to emphasise that in the unprecedented crisis of the interwar period it was the bourgeoisie in the UK which with great tenacity was able to act as a 'class for itself'. There is considerable evidence to suggest that this was not inevitable and that the interests of Department I capitalists did on occasion clash with those of other capitalists—the coal owners were often attacked as being too brutal in their wage cutting. There is also considerable evidence that the combine capitalists were able to manipulate the State apparatus to enforce mergers, cartels, and wage cutting against the opposition of the representatives of labour. More often—and increasingly at the end of the period—the representatives of labour in the Labour Party and unions were in agreement with the policies advocated by the representatives of capital. The combine bourgeoisie, although often on the defensive in the sense that old remedies for falling profits, like wage cutting, did not seem to work any more, nevertheless were repeatedly able to divide the working class by manipulating one coalfield against another. More important, the working class was divided according to the historic experience of the Department I as opposed to the new Department II producers and of course was finely divided through more intimate consumption mechanisms such as housing allocations. (Blacklisting and evictions of militant union men or unemployed workers' leaders were common.)

As noted, in the coalfield areas the progress of recovery after 1937 in Department I production was marked in industries linked to armaments output. However, it was not marked by a rising share of combine output in world markets. Only the stimulus of war demand was strong enough to provoke a return to higher levels of capacity working and employment [5].

[4] Indeed, Richardson (1967) points out that by 1937 the suburbanisation-led boom in the Southeast associated with growth in ownership of houses and other durables was about finished. After that time war demand revived some of the Department I production in some regions and it was this that led 'recovery' from the depression after that date.
[5] The return of 'prosperity' was delayed far longer in many parts of the British empire. In many ways the colonies were most badly retarded by the depression; in Kenya it broke the settler economy.

However, as Heinemann (1944) indicates, in 1942 coal production was still restricted and fell short of the energy requirements of wartime production in the whole economy.

Despite the government's controls, it appeared that quotas, price fixing, and output restrictions were still commonly practised. Moreover, the character of the fixed capital being worked at almost full capacity levels was such as to restrict advances in labour productivity in output terms in the war period. Profits realised in this period (as up to 1919) were not reinvested in new equipment, electrification, and so on, in improving the transportation infrastructure or terminal facilities, or in ways of regulating and improving the health and education provision or other forms of provision for collective or private working-class consumption in the coalfield areas. This applied particularly to even the rudimentary levels of provision necessary for the successful reproduction of (relatively healthy) large masses of semiskilled and semiliterate labour-power in the coalfield areas. Where hospitals had been provided, it had been through voluntary organisations (that is, they were financed out of working-class savings) or through the philanthropy of individual capitalists or landowners.

The underprovision of fixed capital in activities necessary to support a rising level of working-class consumption (indeed to support tolerable minimal conditions for reproduction of labour power on an expanded scale) was of course acutely expressed in the physical condition of working-class housing in the coalfields and in the associated sanitary and other 'neighbourhood' conditions. By the end of a very long period of fluctuating ability to pay for any commodity in large sections of the coalfield working class, coalfield housing was suffering from a similar landlord response: in such unfavourable conditions for the extraction of profits landlords (often the combines or property trusts run by combines) simply tried to extract what they could and avoided any 'unnecessary' expenditures. Despite some local authority provision (in the coalfields most local authorities by the early forties were following the sort of municipal Labourism discussed by Miliband, 1973), the consequences of depressed working-class consumption and private-landlord strategy were such as to provoke massive support for major housing reforms coupled to strong demands for major health reforms, for nationalisation of strategic (mainly combine) industries, and for 'regional' policies to revivify the coalfield areas and continue the experimental transformations of the prewar years—all of which was included in the Labour programme of 1945. Hitherto State involvement in uneven development in the UK space economy had been tentative outside the deployment of the repressive measures necessary to destroy resistance to policies initiated by active capitalists. Now (as indeed in wartime) the State apparatus began to become of *central* importance.

The postwar period: combine transformation, deepening State involvement, and Labourism

Private interests were generally unable in the conditions of the interwar period to run cartels that covered all the major producers in coal, iron and steel, and shipbuilding without the assistance (the 'coordinating' power) of the State. Similarly the combines in 1945 could not undertake the massive new investment required to bring levels of productivity, and levels of replacement of worn-out means of production, transportation, and consumption to a position where even endemic shortages and bottlenecks in strategic industries could be eliminated. By 1946 and 1947, as the winter fuel crises of those years showed, the coal industry was technically incapable of supplying sufficient output to maintain production in the wider economy. Such chronic shortfalls could only be remedied by massive injections of replacement and new investment and by further amalgamations. The combine capitalists had up to 1943 urged that State appropriation of combine means of production should be strongly resisted. Instead they suggested that modernisation of the combine plant and investment in means of transport, etc, could be achieved under further industry-wide employers' associations as set up in the iron and steel industry. Before 1945 combine expenditure on antinationalisation and antisocialist propaganda rose steeply. By 1946 the issue was simply the terms of State compensation for assets to be vested in the State agencies set up to reorganise a good proportion of the branches of production controlled by the combines. There was strong resistance to the nationalisation of *profitable* branches of production during the 1945–1951 period (although by 1975, virtually all the combine production activities were chronically unprofitable and in grave danger of being nationalised). There was also an extremely powerful lobby to destroy any notions of nationalisation without compensation, even if such a policy could have found majority support in Attlee's government. It was not an unreasonable notion, since the first reports of the nationalised industries in the late forties disclosed a condition of chronic unprofitability and the necessity for massive (and in the end crippling) loans to be raised by the State to start coalfield reconstruction.

The terms of compensation, considering the worn-out and unprofitable character of many of the assets nationalised, were wonderfully generous to the interests who had controlled coal (and coal royalties and other coalfield minerals), railway and tramway (and motor bus), gas, water, and electricity companies. Capitalists in the Northeast were allowed a new form of existence on the basis of State compensation. Moreover large portions of the compensation funds were often simply directly transferred to the banks, insurance companies, and finance houses which had lent funds to and frequently 'rescued' combines in the interwar period.

In addition State borrowing to raise sums for compensation payments—
which were in Treasury Stock—and State borrowing to raise funds for
coalfield reconstruction served the interests of finance capital. At this
time finance capital, in the face of competition—from loan funds
originating in the USA—in the international financial system, was seeking
new safe sources of interest payments. As well as this form of competition,
the global hegemony of UK finance capital was also being weakened by
nationalist movements, for example Peron was nationalising UK-owned
assets in Argentina without compensation.

Not only were State loans raised to reconstruct the means of production
in the coalfields, these loans were also raised to reconstruct housing in
such places and especially to support local-authority construction and
experiments in new-town construction[6]. Moreover, State loans were
raised to reconstruct the transport systems in coalfield areas and to
provide all the health and education buildings and services so clearly
lacking in the interwar period. Later, State loans would also be raised to
reconstruct commercial areas in the major coalfield settlements and State
expenditures—both capital and revenue—would be regarded (1964–1970)
as definitive answers to the problem of regional disparities in the UK.
Throughout the period (that is, 1945–1970) the interests of finance capital
were to dictate the character and pace of State-initiated reconstruction of
the coalfield areas. At several times, however, the interests of finance and
other forms of capital seemed to coincide with those of the great programme
of reforms of the 1945–1951 government and occasionally seemed also to
coincide with the aims of the 1964–1970 Labour government's further
attempts at reforms in transportation and housing reconstruction.

Although much more work remains to be done on the postwar
transformation of the combine companies, it is easy to trace the swift
evolution of combines like Powell Duffryn and William Baird into
wholesaling, transportation (mainly road and shipping), and Department II
production (textiles in the case of William Baird). In the Northeast
coalfield an interesting picture of the transformation of some of the old
coal interests into financial trusts speculating in currencies, raw materials,
and property is emerging. (This will be described in detail in further papers).

As noted, the postwar experience in the coalfields has been one of
continuous advance in the progress of the modernisation of everyday life
brought about to serve the interests of Labourist programmes and finance
capital but also to serve the crucial interests of Department II production.
The conditions of collective and especially of private consumption in the
coalfield areas have been altered so as to allow progressive expansion of
Department II production in the UK. Without State expenditures on the
reconstruction of production, circulation, and consumption in the

[6] For example, Peterlee New Town in County Durham was initiated specifically to solve
the housing crisis in East Durham, to ensure adequate labour supplies for the pits there.

coalfields, even with the return in the fifties for a brief time to full employment in such areas, it is doubtful whether mass consumption could have advanced so quickly.

State expenditures on fixed capital in settlements, which took the form of housing redevelopment, health and education provision, transportation, and water and sewer provision, can be interpreted in part as having involved allocations of expenditures to those parts of the space economy that presented the largest barriers to further accumulation in Department II production. However, the aim was to revolutionise the conditions of working-class consumption (as well as production and circulation) in each part of the UK space economy simultaneously. All regions, whether bearing the worn-out fixed capital of the interwar period or led and dominated by the new consumption-goods output of that period, had to be 'integrated' into the advance of mass consumption to prevent recurring realisation (and later investment) problems in Department II production. Such a simultaneous transformation required State capital expenditures in *each* region (including the Southeast). Yet the inheritance of most seriously worn-out capital stock was located in the former coalfield-combine territories. In the event State expenditures could not be mounted on a sufficiently large scale to ensure more than an extremely superficial transformation of the former coalfield regions' production, circulation, and consumption. This was because State expenditures depended on the State's ability to raise revenue and loans and to bear the losses of unprofitable nationalised industries. There were suddenly too many simultaneous demands for capital expenditure to be coped with even by the large financial powers of the State. The erratic and partial progress of State expenditures in the UK in the separate standard regions can be charted for the late sixties and indicates the inability of these expenditures to 'even out' the regional differences in stocks of fixed capital associated with conditions of working-class consumption which were produced under the social relations reproduced by the combines in the interwar period and even earlier.

However, data from the *Census of Production* (for 1958, 1963, 1968) indicate that growth in various profits indices for industrial production in the time 1958–1968 in the UK standard regions was remarkably similar in each region. This indicates that State expenditure on production restructuring, in keeping the advance in the rate of profit between sectors and regions even and convergent, had perhaps more decisive effects than with respect to working-class consumption. This is to be expected, but is also contradictory in that production modernisation is often achieved (and certainly was in the sixties in the Northeast) by drastic closures of unprofitable branches of activity and the introduction of companies paying low wages, and employing a high proportion of females, thereby narrowing the base for mass consumption in the region (see Carney et al., 1975).

The increasing evidence that production modernisation in the Northeast was not 'solving' the problems of high unemployment and low levels of provision of health, housing, and education for the working class in the region was not accompanied by the rise of a new reforming Labourism such as the movement which culminated in 1945. Rather, working-class politics stagnated in the region. The political and trade-union leadership became firmly enmeshed (not unwillingly) *before* 1939 in State-sponsored organisations aimed at injecting new activity into the Special Areas. In effect it was a politically active part of the combine bourgeoisie who ran the new State organisations before 1939, and during the war they strengthened their position on various production, rent control, and food-allocation committees[7]. In 1943 the capitalists of the Northeast brought out a manifesto for postwar reconstruction of the region, which was endorsed by the trade-union leadership in the region and which was uncannily like the programme of reconstruction that was actually carried out. Through various industrial associations and promotional organisations, as well as membership of New Town and other State agencies introduced into the region, the combine bourgeoisie not only strengthened their position (which when their means of production were appropriated by the State had seemed briefly to be insecure) but also succeeded in obtaining a profound consensus as to the programme of expenditures necessary to solve the problems of the Northeast (and also preserve the interests of the combine bourgeoisie). This was vital since it was Labour local authorities who mainly were, in the sixties, to implement the forms of regional modernisation advocated by the bourgeoisie in the region.

The bourgeoisie of the combines of the period to 1946, in the early 1970s may still be identified very readily in terms of lineages of directorships, shareholdings, and positions of influence in the State apparatus. In our investigations of the postwar period in the Northeast we have been repeatedly impressed by the tenacity of the modern bourgeoisie in the region in maintaining a form of dominance (through active use of the State apparatus). The dominance of the bourgeoisie is markedly enforced by the leadership of the working class in the Northeast through programmes of public expenditure mainly geared to investment of a character designed to further bourgeois interests (rather than, for example, to take large portions of working-class housing out of the operations of the housing market or to support moves towards worker control). However, it is not necessarily the case that the politics of the bourgeoisie, enforced through the State apparatus, were in the ascendent over that whole period. It is in this case a mistake to think that the bourgeoisie 'wins' all its struggles or that Labourism was always a withered movement (in terms of mass membership). It was one of the results of modernisation in the region that Labour politics declined but it is a mistake to think that this was an

[7] This can be seen as part of the broader process of 'the depoliticisation of politics' in which political questions are reduced to technical questions to be solved by disinterested experts.

inevitable progression, although by the early seventies it appeared so in retrospect.

It may be that the conflicts between working-class interests and those of the combines and wider bourgeoisie in other coalfield areas were similar. Preliminary research suggests that Labourism in Yorkshire, South Wales, and Nottinghamshire had by the late sixties many of the features of the politics of Labour in the Northeast.

Concluding remarks

The explanation of interregional uneven development in the UK advanced here is in obvious contrast to orthodox accounts. These tend to stress either the importance of 'the market' in the growth of the Southeast (without explaining how 'the market' shifted from the nineteenth century centres of economic activity) or the declining competitiveness of coalfield industries (without asking how this had come about). These failings stem from the neglect of the conditions of production. On the other hand, we have chosen to stress production and so our explanation focuses on the long- and short-period problems of capital accumulation, the responses to these problems, and the link of both to class relationships. Thus it becomes possible to see the connections between interregional uneven development and crucial aspects of the restructuring of liberal capitalism into late capitalism, such as the crises of profitability and overproduction, the involvement of the State in production, and the fiscal crisis of the State.

Nevertheless, there are aspects of interregional uneven development and the emergence of late capitalism which are not sufficiently illuminated by a study of coal combines. Our current research programme is intended to cope with these aspects. At present we are examining, in particular, the following three themes:

(1) the landed interest and the transfer of surplus value within the domestic UK space economy between 1870 and 1939 in connection with the transformation of London and the Southeast in that period;

(2) the impacts of UK investment overseas, on receiving territories in relation to rates of profit, and the impact of repatriated surplus value on the domestic space economy;

(3) the involvement of overseas originating investment in the post 1945 reconstruction of the Distressed Areas of the interwar period, with reference to State policy.

References

Aldcroft D H, Richardson H W, 1969 *The British Economy 1870-1939* (Macmillan, London)

Carney J G, Hudson R, 1975 "The social uses of social knowledge" paper read to the PTRC Annual Conference, 1975, Warwick University (Planning and Transport Research and Computation, London)

Carney J G, Hudson R, Taylor C, 1975 "Inner city employment situations: the case of the North East" paper read to the Inner City Employment Seminar Series at the Centre for Environmental Studies, London

Harvey G, 1917 *Capitalism in the Northern Coalfield* (a copy of this is held in the Newcastle upon Tyne City Library)

Heinemann M, 1944 *Britain's Coal: a Study of the Mining Crisis* (Labour Research Department, London)

Mandel E, 1975 *Late Capitalism* (New Left Books, London)

Mess H A, 1928 *Industrial Tyneside: A Social Survey* (Ernest Benn, London)

Miliband R, 1973 *Parliamentary Socialism* second edition (Merlin Press, London)

Richardson H W, 1967 *Economic Recovery in Britain, 1932–1939* (Weidenfeld and Nicholson, London)

Multinationals, Spatial Inequalities, and Workers' Control

OONAGH McDONALD, M.P.¶
House of Commons

The growth of multinationals and their impact on the economy

The purpose of this paper is to examine the relationship between multinational enterprises and spatial inequalities, and the extent to which workers' control both can act as a countervailing power to the power of multinational companies and can minimise regional inequalities. A multinational manufacturing company is defined as one which produces in at least one foreign country as well as its home country. But, however international its operations may be, a multinational company is not normally multinational in its ownership. Ownership and control are firmly located in a single company. More interestingly, the multinational corporation has been defined as "an organization which, while remaining in private hands, transcends national boundaries and national regulation" (*Interplay*, 1968, page 15).

The total value of the net assets of foreign companies in the UK at the end of 1972 was £3800 million, whereas the total value of overseas investments by UK companies was £8070 million (including oil, insurance, and banking). The latter, in other words, was more than twice the former, representing a debilitating loss of investment capital, increased by the UK's continuing membership of the EEC. UK multinationals are second only to those of the US in the scale of their multinational activities, and they account for about one-fifth of world foreign investment. At the end of 1972 there were about 3000 companies operating in the UK which were controlled by foreign companies. US companies accounted for more than two-thirds of the £3800 million manufacturing and other assets. The value of US-controlled assets was shown as £2448 million, or 64% of the total in the Department of Trade and Industry's survey; companies based on Switzerland came next with 7·5%, and then Canada with 7·0%, and the Netherlands with 15·7%. French, Swedish, Italian, and West German companies accounted for about 2% each (*Trade and Industry*, 15th November 1973). But, since US multinationals sometimes own UK holding companies, the US stake in British manufacturing industry must be higher than 64%, of the total foreign investment.

The proportion of UK manufacturing industry owned and controlled by foreign multinationals has been increasing since World War II. In 1970 it was about 16% and had been rising by just over half a percentage point each year. If this trend continues, the share of foreign multinationals will reach 20% before 1980. This stake is very unevenly distributed

¶ Member of the Association of Scientific, Technical, and Managerial Staffs (ASTMS).

between industries, being especially concentrated in the most technologically advanced and rapidly growing sections.

The most important share of foreign investment in UK manufacturing industries is, obviously, American and any study of the impact of foreign investment in the UK, especially at the regional level, must examine the role of US investment specifically. Dunning (1972) gives a detailed picture of the extent of US investment in the UK, and some features of this are worth noting, since they indicate the degree of the contribution to industrial concentration made by US companies. Thus in 1970–1971 US affiliates in UK manufacturing industries sold goods worth nearly £6000 million, nearly 13% of the total production of all UK manufacturing enterprises. US investment employs 9·2% of the UK labour force and accounts for 20% of all UK manufacturing exports.

The US stake in UK manufacturing industry has increased rapidly since 1950. Between 1950 and 1970 the direct capital stake of US companies in the UK grew on average by 12%, that is, nearly twice the rate of growth of the GNP. By 1970 there were over 2000 US affiliates operating in the UK, four out of five of which were 100% US-owned. Of the 500 largest US manufacturing affiliates in the UK in 1970–1971, the top three accounted for 25% of the total sales, and 27% of the total capital employed: the corresponding proportions for the top ten and the top twenty companies were 43% and 50%, and 54% and 65%, respectively. US affiliates exported nearly 25% of their output in 1970–1971—a much higher proportion than that of the average UK firm. Slightly more than half of their exports went to other parts of the enterprise of which the affiliates were a part, so that Europe was the main market. Little information on the imports of the affiliates is available, although it is known that they imported goods and services equal to 5·6% of their sales in 1966. In view of this volume, US affiliates must have a significant impact on the UK balance of payments.

In the last two decades, US manufacturing affiliates in the UK have earned a consistently higher rate of return on their capital than have their UK competitors. The gap is narrowing and it appears that US affiliates are more sensitive to cyclical fluctuations. However, an analysis of accounts for 1970–1971 show that in 67% of the industries in which they operate, with notable exceptions, such as motor vehicle manufacturers, US affiliates record a higher profitability than UK firms. US affiliates used labour and capital more productively than their UK competitors, at least in 36 out of 39 industrial groups surveyed in 1970–1971. As compared with UK firms, labour productivity was 33% higher and their rate of return on sales was more than half as much again as that of UK firms.

This kind of performance probably accounts for their faster rate of growth, compared with their UK competitors. Between 1957 and 1968 the scale of their output increased by 339% compared with 178% for all UK firms. This reflects both the increased numbers of US affiliates and the fact

70 O.McDonald

that they tend to be more concentrated than UK firms in the fast-growing industries, and in the more research intensive and technologically advanced sections of the industry.

In fact, US participation in UK industry is to be found in only a small number of industrial sectors. Some 60% of the sales, and more than 50% of the employment is in food, tobacco, mineral oil refining, metal manufacturing, instrument engineering, other electronic apparatus, and motor vehicle manufacturing (Dunning, 1972, page 4). These same sectors account for 38% of the sales and 28% of the employment of all UK companies (including US affiliates). Within these sectors the share of US affiliates varies considerably, from, for example, 90% of sales in photographic and copying equipment, to 68% of sales in electronic computers, and less than 1% in the drinks trade. Overall, US affiliates clearly play an important part in the UK economy, indeed a dominant role in trading, sales, and R and D in some sectors, and they are responsible for job opportunities for a majority of employees in certain industries.

The tendency in the UK over recent years has been for more and more economic activity to become concentrated in a relatively few large firms, and it is arguable that foreign direct investment in the UK has contributed to this process. At the aggregate level, the hundred largest firms in UK manufacturing industry accounted for 20% of net output in 1948. By 1970 it was 45%–50%. The hundred largest companies in the industrial and commercial sector increased their share of total net assets from 47% in 1948 to 51% in 1957 and 64% in 1968. The top one hundred manufacturing firms in Britain now control one-half of net manufacturing output, compared with one-fifth in 1950. At industry level there was a sharp increase in concentration in the UK between 1958 and 1963. The average five-firm sales concentration for 209 products increased from 54·4% in 1958 to 58·9% in 1963. An increase in concentration occurred in 67% of the products, whereas only 32% showed a decline. The industry groups in which increases in concentration were especially marked were food and drink, vehicles, textiles and leather, clothing, and footwear. These, together with electrical engineering, largely coincided with those in which merger activity was intense in the 1960s. The trend in concentration in these industries continued throughout that decade.

The increase in concentration has come about partly as a result of an accelerating merger rate since the mid-1950s. Mergers are the prime cause of the increase in concentration between 1958 and 1967 (Aaronovitch and Sawyer, 1975). With the intensification of merger activity after 1965 it is probable that the rate of increase in business concentration has also increased. But, although the emphasis on mergers seems reasonable, it may have to be qualified when the differential internal growth of enterprises is measured. Between 1958 and 1963 mergers and the differential internal growth of enterprises had approximately equal effects in increasing concentration ratios within Census of Production groups.

Both of these forms of increasing concentration suggest that foreign investment played its part in bringing about the present situation. This seems to be borne out by an examination of some of the case histories described by Walshe (1974). (Since the 1963 census publishes product concentration ratios, we are here studying market rather than industrial structures.) Thus Standard Telephones and Cables (STC), General Electric (GEC), Telephone Manufacturing Company (acquired by Pye in 1960), and Siemens [acquired by Amalgamated Electrical Industries (AEI) in 1954] were the only major firms in telegraphic and telephone installations and electronics when tendering for the Post Office contract began in 1964. STC originally established its position by its ability to exploit (or acquire exclusive UK rights in) new inventions. Only during the 1960s have mergers played a significant part in increasing concentration in telecommunications. Plessey merged with Automatic Telephones and Electric, and with Ericsson Telephones in 1961, whereas the GEC, AEI–English Electric combine was formed in 1967–1968. These mergers had the effect of reducing the number of major firms on the exchange sector to three; but with Plessey expanding in the field at this time, the number of major firms in line apparatus remained at four.

Tobacco products provide another example of a product made under conditions of monopoly or near monopoly. The cigar market is dominated by Gallaher, which increased its market share initially through acquisitions such as that of J R Freeman and Sons (a Cardiff firm) in 1947, and Richard Lloyd and Sons in 1953, and subsequently through internal growth. The demise of small firms and the dominance of large firms is related to economies of scale, mergers, the ability to introduce new products in bulk, advertising and market economics, and easier access to capital for investment in the latest cigar-making technology. This trade, like the cigarette trade, had production shares frozen by import controls in the mid-1950s. Under these conditions larger firms could grow only by acquisition, as did Gallaher. After the mid-1950s smaller firms were gradually eliminated by the external growth policy of larger firms, which controlled about 80% of the imports, having in the past successfully evaded import controls by acquisition. In 1970–1971, Gallaher's sales totalled £436393 million with exports of £2392 million and capital employed of £121641 million (Dunning, 1972; Table 1:29).

These examples indicate that foreign investment, especially US investment, may have had a significant part to play in the increase in concentration in UK manufacturing industry, both through processes of internal growth and through external expansion by mergers. Comprehensive data on the methods by which US firms gain a stake in UK industry are not at present available. An investigation of 205 US affiliates established in the UK in the mid-1950s showed that only 20% of them had involved a takeover or partial takeover of UK interests. The rest had been set up as new subsidiaries. Purchases or part-purchases of existing UK companies have become rather more common both as a means of initial entry into the UK market and as a way of extending the activities of established US affiliates: examples include the Chrysler investment in Rootes in 1966, the Litton Imperial Typewriter takeover in 1966, and General Mills' purchase of the Smith Ford Group in 1967. In 1969–1971 there were altogether 72 acquisitions of UK companies by all foreign concerns.

Where such purchases or takeovers occur, it seems that they lead to total US ownership rather than to joint ventures. Dunning's researches into 500 leading affiliates in 1970 suggests that 83% of assets in 1970–1971 were 100% subsidiaries of US companies, whereas in only 63 affiliates was there any long-term debt capital held by the US company. 100% ownership is more common in high-technology than in low-technology industries, in ventures established since 1955 than in those set up before 1939, in US affiliates rather than in other foreign affiliates, and in the UK rather than elsewhere. In 1967 the proportion of large US affiliates in all activities in the UK which were wholly owned (69%) was higher than in most countries of the world (including France and Germany).

The result for the UK is that there is a marked concentration of US participation in the more research-intensive and technologically advanced sectors of UK industry. In 1968 79·7% of the capital stake of US affiliates and 66·8% of their sales was in these sectors. The corresponding share of the net assets of the leading UK companies was 45·3% and the proportion of sales of all manufacturing industries was 39·5% (cf Dunning, 1972, tables 1:3, 1:14, 1:15). However, between 1957 and 1968 the share of the total sales of US affiliates in the research-intensive sectors increased only slightly, and in three of the five sectors, that is, chemicals and allied products, mechanical and electrical engineering vehicles, and rubber products the concentration coefficient, that is, the share of UK sales of goods produced in the UK, manufactured by a small number (normally five) of leading firms, has fallen. This is partly because of the number of takeovers in paper, metal manufacturing, and other manufacturing sectors, and the divestment of the interest of General Telephones and Electronics in Thorn Electrical, but mainly because of the faster growth of UK companies in the technologically advanced sectors. In all industries, the participation of US affiliates has risen and, apart from those in food and rubber sectors, it has risen substantially. Even here, the participation of US affiliates in food, drink, and tobacco has increased since 1968.

Explanations of the reasons for direct investment abroad, and in particular US investment abroad, are complex. But an important part of the explanation for a company's going multinational is to be found in their monopoly situations in the home market. Large firms, especially in America, can support major research programmes from their dominant position at home. When the market in new products abroad has been by direct export, it becomes profitable for the firm to invest directly and start production abroad. The direct investor "begins in a position of

monopoly at home, and continues in a monopolistic position abroad ...
it suggests the importance to the phenomenon of a continually maintained
monopoly position achieved in a continually advancing R and D
programme" (Steuer, 1971, page 72). Where foreign subsidiaries are part
of this innovatory process, their market share in a particular year is
unlikely to be a good guide to their monopoly power. If they are not in
the top five firms, they are likely to erode the concentration level in
their industry. And if they are already amongst the top five firms in their
industry, concentration is likely to increase. Thus 51 of the largest
500 companies operating in the UK are foreign subsidiaries, which
suggests that they are likely to be amongst the largest firms in their
respective industries. The effects of multinationals are complex, but foreign
subsidiaries are probably in stronger competitive positions than their market
shares suggest. Thus Dunning's analyses probably do not indicate the
strength and significance of US investment in UK manufacturing industry.

Other reasons for the outward flow of US investment should not be
neglected. It has already been argued that this flow arises from a near
monopoly, or oligopolistic position, and from a sound basis of advanced
technology, in which it becomes increasingly expensive for a large firm to
increase its share of the market. In the US, a rigorous antitrust policy
has made it more and more difficult to increase market power by means
of horizontal and vertical mergers. Going multinational is a way of
avoiding such laws. By contrast, although British companies have faced
weak antitrust laws "they have been less inclined to compete ... than the
Americans ... . They have therefore resorted, to a much greater extent,
to all sorts of restrictive agreements as their means of maintaining an
equilibrium with the environment (George and Silberston, 1975, page 185).
From this secure basis, British companies also went multinational to
ensure markets for their products abroad.

The impact of multinationals on the economy as a whole should also
be noted. To a large extent this is a matter of interpreting the *financial*
strategies of multinational companies. Foreign-owned subsidiaries remit
their earnings to their owners through dividends, royalties, fees, interest,
and trade; royalties and fees being in principle payment for specific
goods or services received by the subsidiary. But, since many of these
have no easily determined market value, companies have considerable
latitude to charge a fair arm's length value to the subsidiaries, and, since
such payments are a before-tax charge against profits, some companies
prefer to substitute these for dividends. Transfer pricing provides
multinationals with important additional means of transferring funds and
earnings in pursuit of various corporate objectives. Such a system works
by the arbitrary pricing of intracompany transfers of goods and services
at a higher or lower figure than the value received. Transfer prices can be
used to minimise the tax burden, to avoid the effects of currency
devaluation, or to limit exchange losses where chronic inflation or balance

of payment difficulties are a continual threat. Plainly these operations could have a substantial impact on a government's policies to deal with balance of payment difficulties. Transfer pricing can also be used to provide a foreign subsidiary with finance, to give a new subsidiary a competitive advantage by pricing imports low, or to give it a greater profit margin. This method can also be used to understate profits which might otherwise induce customers to ask for price reductions or unions to ask for wage increases.

An interesting feature of many multinationals is their attempt to integrate closely their world operating facilities. In intermediate-technology trades, each operating subsidiary in each country is more likely to produce the whole, and similar, products. But a much more international division of labour exists in high-technology industries, sometimes vertically, with each subsidiary undertaking part of the process of production or supplying a range of components, and sometimes horizontally, with subsidiaries trading foreign products with each other, and sometimes, as with Ford and IBM, a mixture of the two. Thus the advantages of technology may be exported but not shared.

In these ways, the advantages of its developed technology are not lost by the parent company. Furthermore, the subsidiary company is less vulnerable to takeovers in the host country or to state acquisition by the host country. Such operating strategies are undertaken in the context of the global interests of the multinational enterprise, which may conflict with the desired trade flows of the host country. And it is through such strategies that the greatest manipulation of transfer prices occurs. It is here, too, that the conflict of interests between the multinational and the nation state in which it operates is most likely to arise.

In conclusion "whatever the force of technology, it is clear that the growth of multinational corporations, by itself, tends to weaken nation states. Multinational corporations render ineffective many traditional policy instruments, the capacity to tax, to restrict credit, to plan investment, etc., because of their international flexibility. In addition, multinational corporations act as vehicles for the intrusion of the policies of one country into another, with the ultimate effect of lessening the power of both. These tendencies have long been recognised in dependent developing countries, but it is now also evident that even the US as a *nation-state*, is losing some of its 'independence' as it attempts to cope with the tangled web woven by its international business". Thus there is bound to be "a conflict at a fundamental level between national planning by political units, and international planning by corporations that will assume major proportions as direct investment grows" (Hymer and Rowthorn, 1970, pages 88, 90).

Multinationals and spatial inequalities
Some studies seem to suggest that multinationals do not contribute in any significant way to spatial inequalities. A recent study of inward direct investment suggests that "we can expect a disproportionate

tendency for the foreigner to locate a new establishment in more remote regions". The reasons for this belief are that "economic criteria such as cheaper land with opportunities for expansion, and an ample supply of labour probably receive a heavier weighting for the foreign than for the domestic investor. Also our preliminary statistical information enables us to hazard the generalisation that foreign direct investment is more concentrated in light manufacturing and science-based industry. There are likely to be instances where location is less predetermined by the necessity of being near particular sources of raw materials and transport facilities. The latter point follows from the characteristically high ratio of the volume or product to transport cost in the newer incoming industries. These factors all point to location away from the more congested areas of the south, especially around London." This line of reasoning leads the authors to expect the "pattern" of new establishments in the more remote regions "to become more pronounced over time" (Steuer et al, 1973, page 105).

The figures given in table 1 are intended to give some picture of foreign-directed activity, though, since foreign investment is on the whole concentrated in capital-intensive, science-based industries, they probably underestimate the importance of foreign-owned firms in a region. Other studies relating to US investment in manufacturing industry give the same impression. US manufacturing affiliates employed nearly 730000 people in 1970–1971 in the UK and of these, less than 0·2% were US nationals, though this figure rises to 2% for managerial employees. Nevertheless, in three out of four US affiliates the managing director was found to be British. US subsidiaries not only employed a substantial number of workers but on average paid them higher wages. In 1970–1971 US affiliates paid 23% more wages and salaries per employee than UK firms (£29.06 v £23.48 per week), though the payroll costs per employee are lower than comparable affiliates operating on the Continent (Dunning, 1972, page 5).

What is the distribution of employment by US affiliates? In 1967 the activities of about half the leading American affiliates in the UK were located in London and the South East, and one in three in the least prosperous regions. Within these latter regions the Development Areas

Table 1. The percentage of total regional employment in foreign-owned manufacturing establishments. (Source: Steuer et al, 1973, page 197.)

Region	%	Region	%
Yorkshire and North Humber	2·5	East Midlands	3·3
East Anglia	11·2	South East	12·4
South West	1·2	Wales	8·5
West Midlands	4·1	North West	5·6
Scotland	7·2	Northern England	4·5
UK	6·8		

were host to 125 of the 270 industrial affiliates which supplied
information to the American Chamber of Commerce in 1971. In 1970
these firms employed 124 727 people or 28·1% of the total number
employed in the sample: Scotland attracted 40% of this employment and
North West England 33%. Between 1945 and 1965, of the 250 foreign-
owned establishments (mainly US) setting up plants in the UK, 76
(employing 46 000) went to Scotland, 46 (employing 17 000) went to South
East England, 32 (employing 10 000) went to the North West, 22 (employing
8000) went to Northern Ireland, 24 (employing 9000) went to Wales, 5000
jobs went to North East England, and the balance to other parts of England.
It is therefore claimed that, through this injection of new capital and
technology, upwards of 150 000 jobs have been directly or indirectly created
in the Development Areas, many new industries established, new skills
introduced and local economies strengthened and stabilised (Dunning, 1972,
page 12).

But against this assessment should be set Dunning's (1969; 1972, page 13)
own map which indicates that there were 454 US companies located in the
South East as against, for example, 25 in Wales, and 29 in Northern England,
and no more than 94 in any other region of the UK. This picture of the
distribution of US companies suggests that Dunning's assessment of the
contribution made by US investment to the lessening of regional inequalities
in employment may be overoptimistic. Certainly much more needs to be
known about the size of the US establishments and the number and type of
personnel employed, and no true assessment of the contribution of foreign,
and especially American, investment to regional unemployment can be
made without this sort of detailed information and analysis.

A similar criticism applies to a recent article by Evans (1973) in which
the author investigates the pattern of head-office location and argues that
the concentration of head offices of large companies and particularly the
national offices of foreign-owned subsidiaries is counterbalanced by the
growth of other companies within small towns and regions and the location
of their head offices away from London. Evans argues, "if we examine
the existing companies at any date within the period [1965–1968] we
may find no centralisation because new companies have come into
existence and it is plausible to assume that these companies will be
distributed in more or less the same way as the population" (page 393).
Evans concludes that, if there has been any increase in centralisation
between 1965 and 1968, it has been slight. The whole argument,
however, neglects certain important features of regional inequalities.
It is not just the number and distribution of establishments such as head
offices, but the number of people employed, the type of employment
available in the head office, and the operations demanded of the
employees, plus the possibility of further employment being generated by
the head office, which are the relevant considerations. Once these aspects
are taken into account, the whole argument may be destroyed.

The possibility exists, though, of directing foreign investment to depressed regions, and, when foreign-owned establishments are located in regions of Britain where economic activity is depressed and where the level of unemployment is high, the potential gains seem very great. The exact nature of the contribution made by foreign direct investment calls for examination, which should go beyond numbers employed by subsidiary companies and overall comparative wage levels. For example, the Department of Trade and Industry survey, which included a brief excursion to Greenock, points out that IBM, the dominant employer, does not draw its employees from the ranks of the unemployed, nor from school leavers, since IBM offers little training. What the company requires is "the right sort of person; someone who will fit in with the task required, learn a specific skill relatively easily ... the advantage of hiring people who have acquired their general training elsewhere is partly the saving on training, and partly the greater knowledge one has of what the worker is like" (Steuer et al, 1973, page 112).

Similar features were observed about Ford's recruitment policy at Halewood: Ford "aimed to recruit from the 'cream of the labour market' and although the rate of pay it offered was lower than at Dagenham and significantly lower than the rates operating in the Midlands, the state of the labour market at Merseyside made it high enough to serve the company's purpose. Family men with commitments came first. Stable men who were tied down with debt and responsibility were given priority. Men under twenty were formally barred and there was little welcome at Halewood for men off the docks or [from] the building [trade] ... . Neither were the unemployed welcome." And "the reasons which influenced the Ford Motor Company's move to Halewood were the same as led it to establish a plant at Genk in the underdeveloped region of Belgium. Unemployment means low wages and a vulnerable labour force" (Beynon, 1973, pages 89, 65).

Seen in this light, the contribution made by multinational companies to underdeveloped regions in terms of employment and the acquisition of skills is more limited than it might first appear. Typically they offer little by way of training, and the skills they employ are often very limited in scope, not easily transferable by the worker to other companies or types of employment. Creaming off the labour market makes it more difficult for UK industries to develop in the regions. And finally, although wage levels may be higher than those offered by UK companies in the area, they do not equal those in the more prosperous regions of the UK.

The contribution made by the multinational companies to the problems of regional unemployment depends also on the distribution of operating and control units. Such units, especially control units, are likely to be concentrated in London and the South East, although regional disparities decline from the group head office, to the central services, to research and development, to divisional head offices, the last control group being twice as concentrated as the operating units. This kind of regional distribution coupled with the corporate policies of multinational enterprise sharpens regional disparities. These companies tend to use their professional services, located at head office or in specialist divisions, rather than local labour near the factory, to hire maintenance labour from within the company, and to centre purchasing decisions about capital equipment and raw materials at head office, making it unlikely that such purchases will take place at the local factory. These policies tend in turn to reduce local spending through a decline in the regional wage packet, leading to a decline in regional consumption. Further, providing specialist facilities on a national basis may increase the level of regional imports. Altogether, such corporate policies lead to a fall in the level of local income (based on Parsons, 1971).

Such are the continuing regional inequalities which arise from the hiring, wages, and planning policies of the multinational companies. It is moreover unlikely that they will be reversed by government policies of grants and tax concessions. Financial incentives can mean little to multinationals with access to low-cost labour in less-developed countries. These costs can be as low as a quarter of the price of labour in the UK Development Areas, so that, to compete, the Regional Employment Premium (REP) would have to be raised to 75% of labour costs in the UK. This was affirmed by evidence given to a House of Commons Expenditure Committee by multinational companies. Unilever said "We are unable to produce evidence from our own experience that REP has increased investment or employment in Development Areas", and Univac stated "We would have gone to a Development Area regardless of the grants offered" (Commons Expenditure Committee, 1973).

Furthermore, multinational companies are in a position to bargain about the location of their establishments. They are in a position to demand Industrial Development Certificates, as, for example, with IBM's claim that they needed to establish their new plant at Havant to be nearer their research establishment. Unfettered by current location restrictions, and unmoved by government financial incentives, the multinational company is free to decide where to invest its capital—whether to expand or contract its production in this country or that, and how much is to be spent on plant and machinery in each country.

Workers' control
The preceding discussion gives some indication of the concentration of resources and power in multinational companies. It is difficult for governments to curtail these powers, nor are there adequate checks in the operation of the market. The most marked departures from 'acceptable market performance' occur in industries with very high levels of

concentration and high entry barriers to new competition—typically markets in which multinational companies operate. Nor does there appear to be any adequate countervailing power in the UK. Scherer has discussed such power in the American economy and finds the opposite to be true: "Buyers may be able to exploit their power to secure lower intermediate product prices, and they may pass on the resultant savings to consumers" (Scherer, 1971, page 252). Furthermore, monopoly legislation plays no real part in the UK in restraining multinationals or in decreasing concentration. In general, the various interrelated elements in the multinational challenge to economic sovereignity include the undermining of fiscal, monetary, and regional policy, the partial obliteration of exchange-rate variation as an instrument of trade policy, exchequer loss, balance-of-payment losses, and inflationary pressure, and, finally, the ever-present threat of extranational location if they are not allowed location in the region of their choice. It is therefore necessary to harness the power of big business and ensure that it fulfills social and economic policies. Can workers' control, as a more representative countervailing power, fulfill this function?

The organisation of workers' representatives at company level is a major challenge, posing an unprecedented threat to established organisations in the giant companies. Some of these companies employ over 100000 people in the private sector. And in many cases, leading private companies are themselves holding companies for a wide range of subsidiary enterprises of considerable size. This could well mean conflicts of interest between workers for subsidiary companies in the same group, and also conflicts of interest between different groups of workers in the same industry. Therefore any form of workers' control must be sufficiently complex to match the complexity of the organisation concerned, sufficiently skillful and flexible to meet the demands of large-scale organisation and to cope with such clashes between groups of workers when they occur.

But the crucial aspect of the power of multinationals which the workers must control is the power of the multinational over investment decisions. This is the power which strengthens management against the workers in a multinational enterprise. Capital is much more mobile than labour, and multinationalisation has further facilitated this mobility, so that the job security of workers employed by multinationals is lessened, and bargaining power vis-à-vis management is weakened. Thus, for example, in September 1973 Chrysler threatened to sack 8000 of its workers in Coventry and to cut down investments in the UK if disputes with the trade unions were not settled quickly. More usually, it is said that new investment will be switched to another country. During the 1971 Ford strike the managing director wrote to the *Times* (23rd February) stating that his company last week decided to recommend the US parent company "against expenditure of almost £30m for a major expansion project".

And according to the *Financial Times* (26th September 1973) Ford
expanded its engine manufacturing company in Brazil instead of in the
UK largely because of the 1971 strike.

Whatever form workers' participation takes within the structure of a
particular company, it must involve the trade union movement. This is
the first prerequisite of an adequate counterbalance to multinationals.
Involving the trade unions will go part of the way towards enabling
workers to meet the demands placed upon them to match the organisation
of a multinational company. Trade unions would possess certain
organisational skills, and more important, would be able to draw on
resources and consultants in the trade union movement outside the
company. Further, trade unionists involved in some form of workers'
control—joint committees or councils for example—would be able to draw
on the strength of the trade union movement, organised through shop
steward combine committees in a particular company or industry, on a
multiregional, and increasingly on a multinational, basis.

In this context the strengthening of links between national unions
through the International Trade Secretariats, with which many British
trade unions are affiliated, and which are formed under the auspices of
the International Federation of Free Trade Unions with which the TUC
is affiliated, has a vital role to play. Examples of the former are the
International Metalworkers' Federation, the International Federation of
Chemical and General Workers' Unions, and the International Graphical
Federation. Some of these have helped to set up standing groups, such
as the Autoworkers Councils for Ford and General Motors, and the many
multinational company councils set up by the International Federation of
Chemical and General Workers' Union. It is only in this way that any
form of workers' participation can hope to match the power of
management of multinationals, depending as it does, *inter alia*, on the
mobility of capital.

Many multinational companies, perhaps out of a certain sensitivity to
the political and social consequences of their presence in the host
country, but more probably for other reasons, are prepared to consider
certain forms of worker participation. Sometimes, as in the case of
Chrysler earlier this year, trade unions are asked to produce a scheme for
worker participation. Such requests for participation, or proposals for
certain forms of it, require careful and cautious examination, especially
where the proposed scheme entails some form of joint consultative
committees.

The method of joint consultation is the approach about which the
workers are most likely to be canvassed by the multinational companies.
This method was originally introduced in the UK just after the First
World War, but the number and importance of these joint production or
joint consultation committees declined rapidly with the collapse of the
postwar boom in 1920-1921. However, during World War II there was

a widespread rediscovery of joint consultation, leading to joint production committees in which works managers, engineers, and foremen sat alongside shop stewards and discussed the whole range of production problems as well as the traditional issues of welfare and so on. Owing to the universal commitment to the war effort, the growth of these committees did not serve to question control and authority in industry. After the war the influence of joint production committees waned, and joint consultation was officially encouraged, especially in the nationalised industries. But by the early 1950s there was widespread disillusion amongst workers about its effectiveness. This disillusion was due less to the apathy of the workers than to the limited range, not to say the triviality, of the issues available for consultation. Joint consultation committees slowly faded out of existence, since they were clearly ineffective bodies.

The forms of worker participation now being proposed cover both joint consultation committees of some kind or possibly worker representatives on boards of directors, an idea which is sometimes warmly welcomed by industrialists. An editorial article in the *Director* (the Journal of the Institute of Directors) in March 1967 stated (page 7): "The idea of getting workers on to the boards of directors is now beginning to develop a notable head of steam ... . The Government wants the unions to share the responsibility for some of the expected unpopular decisions" (in this case, redundancies in the steel industry). The purpose of such participation is simply to make unpalatable decisions acceptable. This can be seen even more clearly in a description of plant meetings. At such meetings the management's aim is to achieve engineered outbursts of cooperation from hitherto cooperative workers, those who, for various reasons used to make 'helpful' suggestions before the deal. What management want is "to move towards a situation in which, ideally, all their workers are like this, and again ideally, every day, not just at plant meetings. Their industrial heaven is one in which workers are not just interested in the particular organisation of their own work but are firmly identified with the purpose and organisation of production at plant, site and company level" (Nichol, 1975)[1].

Thus certain kinds of worker participation may not in any way serve as a countervailing power to that of the multinational companies, but may instead weaken the existing counterbalance of trade union organisation. Participation may well not offer any real power-sharing.

[1] This approach to the attitudes of management should be contrasted with that of the Department of Trade and Industry's study in which it was noted that IBM had carried out a survey amongst their employees about their attitudes towards trade unionism. The survey was said to have shown that relations with the majority of employees would have been less good if trade unions had been involved in negotiations at the plant. The authors conclude "The very act of conducting an elaborate survey of its employees is indicative of management foresight and attention given to personnel matters" (Steuer et al, 1973, page 115).

For even the beginning of an adequate countervailing power, the proposed participatory structure must include the trade unions, and it must also involve access to the affairs of the multinational company. Workers must be capable of anticipating decisions, especially investment decisions, which are not taken at plant level. The 'books' must be opened so that feasibility studies can be carried out in advance of decisions. If the information required for participation is to be in any way effective, it must at least cover methods of production, production programmes and manpower planning.

Real involvement of all the workers in a particular company must imply control and in some cases this must be on an industry-wide basis. The difficulties inherent in planning the form worker control should take are formidable. There can be no blueprint for the structure of this control, since it will inevitably be related to, if not dependent on, the nature of the industry concerned. One such attempt to work out a plan for workers' control was made recently by the Bristol Aircraft Workers (1974).

A brief description of their proposals will help us to see the form which workers' control may take. The structure suggested matches the present organisation of a privately-owned multiregional or multinational firm with both centralisation and a certain devolution of responsibility. The Bristol scheme envisaged a controlling council at industry level, elected from and by trade unionists working in the industry. The council would work at industry level and would be responsible for the broad policy of the industry. It would be responsible for the appointment and dismissal of all members of the Industry Management Executive, a professional management body which would implement and give detailed substance to the overall policy decisions of the controlling council, be responsible for day-to-day management decisions and the appointment of regional/divisional and plant management executives.

The aim of these proposals is also to ensure that those who work in the industry have a real sense of involvement in the decisions which affect their working lives. It would therefore be necessary to create an environment at shop and office level in which workers will want to use their talents. At plant level there would be joint trade union committees to negotiate with the plant management, and specialist trade union committees to deal with issues such as safety. These proposals go further than the current TUC ones which simply allow for 50% trade union representation on boards of publicly owned industries, the trade union representatives to be nominated by the TUC (TUC, 1974). The latter proposals do not give scope for real involvement of the workers of an industry in decisionmaking, and the nomination, rather than the election, of trade union representatives on boards does not make them accountable to those who work in the industry.

But the possibility of this kind of workers' control can be realised in the multinational context only if the subsidiary of the firm in question passes into public ownership. Even a more effective, though less extensive, kind of worker participation than those described earlier may well presuppose the host company's having a share in equity.

It is often argued that the questions of ownership and control are now quite separate; that the ownership of a multinational company is quite irrelevant and that only managerial strategy demands consideration. Thus, for example, as Galbraith points out, the fact that "the power in the mature corporation passes from the stockholder to the management has long been conceded ... . And increasingly, it is accepted that the goals of management may be distinct from those of the owners ... there will be greater concern for the reliability of revenues, and especially for the growth of the firm. The separation of ownership from control involves a sharp challenge to the assumption of profit maximization (Galbraith, 1974, page 90). This, Galbraith argues, has been a more substantial change than many realise. It is not simply that the corporation aims for some combination of security, growth, and profit, and that prices are a little lower, and sales a little larger, than if profits were exclusively the goal. The point is that "with the rise of the great corporations goes the power extensively to force its will on society—not only to fix prices and costs but to influence consumers, and organize the supply of materials and components, and mobilize its own savings and capital, and develop a strategy for handling labour and influence the attitudes of the community and the actions of the state—then the purposes of its controlling intelligence, of its technostructure become of the highest importance" (page 91). Its purposes, it is argued, are to perpetuate its own existence and to preserve its power—purposes which can clash with those of the owners of the company, if indeed the latter were allowed to interfere with the running of the company. It is possible, however, that the rift between the two sets of purposes has been overemphasised, and that management, at a conscious level at least, identifies much more closely with the purposes of the owners of capital.

However, be that as it may, the *apparent* rift has led some to argue that ownership is no longer relevant. "Ownership of the means of production [is] no longer the key factor" which imparts to society "its essential character" (Crosland, 1974). But democratisation of the giant and multinational companies, especially given the dominance of the technostructure, obviously means a radical change in the organisation of a multinational company. The change is radical even where the proposed democratisation of the company is slight. It is difficult to see how such change can be brought about apart from a change in ownership, from the extension of public ownership. Public ownership is a necessary, but not a sufficient, condition of workers' control.

It is sometimes felt that workers' control could never match the
smooth and decisive organisation of a multinational company. But this
is to underestimate the clash of opposing forces in the decisionmaking
process, between the financial interests of the parent company and those
of the subsidiary, and perhaps the host country as well; between the
nationally orientated and internationally minded members of the group;
between the demands for local autonomy and the demands for central
control. There may also be conflicts between the various groups within
the company, that is, product groups and regional and central service
groups. There are many possible sources of conflict and of divergencies
of policy which can curtail the efficiency of the enterprise at present.
Further, the direction of the enterprise by senior management can be
undermined by professional links across national frontiers fostered by
ease of communications and international conferences. These are likely
to become more significant in the future, and enable both the rapid
transmission of ideas from one country to another, and the forging of
horizontal links within the multinational organisation, which could serve
as a challenge to central management. The advantage of workers' control
is that the possibility of such conflicts of interest can be brought out
into the open and incorporated where possible into the strategy of the
enterprise.

However, not only can conflicts of interest arise in the organisation,
and possibly disrupt its smooth running, but the company can often be
wasteful of its human resources. The attempts to ensure central control
can lead to a waste of management resources, and especially the
underemployment of senior management in the host country. The latter
are often strained in a conflict situation in which they are expected to be
loyal to the parent company and yet naturally identify to some extent
with the interests of the subsidiary company. Such strains can appear
at all levels of management. The purpose of workers' control is to
harmonise and exploit the talents of all employees in company or industry.

The difficulties facing any programme of democratisation and
humanisation of a giant corporation, or even of a subsidiary of a
multinational company, are immense. Any serious programme of
democratisation depends on the introduction of at least an element of
public ownership. The problem here is, as Steuer points out (pages
168-169), that in "taking over a subsidiary of an international company
one is not necessarily purchasing a viable economic entity". This is
partly due to the international division of labour existing within the
company, where a nationally based subsidiary may be producing only
integral components of a final product which is assembled elsewhere.
Further, the location of the essential backup programme of research and
development may be located in the country of origin of the multinational
company, while "by reducing effective options open to a host government,

technological dependence does lead to a reduction in national sovereignity" (Steuer et al, 1973, pages 168–169). This means that the problems of democratisation and a proper regional distribution of employment and income in industry cannot be tackled in isolation from other government economic policies, including encouraging proper and full-scale research and development programmes.

References
Aaronovitch S, Sawyer M C, 1975 "Mergers, growth and concentration" *Oxford Economic Papers* **27** (1) 136–155
Beynon H, 1973 *Working for Ford* (Penguin/Allen Lane, Harmondsworth)
Bristol Aircraft Workers, 1974 *A New Approach to Public Ownership* Institute of Workers' Control, pamphlet number 43, Institute of Workers' Control, Nottingham, England
Commons Expenditure Committee, 1973 *Second Report—Regional Development Incentives, Minutes of Evidence*, published 1974 as HC 85-1 (HMSO, London)
Crosland A, 1974 *Socialism Now and Other Essays* (Jonathan Cape, London)
Dunning J H, 1969 *The Role of American Investment in the British Economy* PEP Broadsheet number 507 (PEP, London)
Dunning J H, 1972 *United States Industry in Britain, 1970–1971* (*Financial Times*, London)
Evans A W, 1973 "The location of the headquarters of industrial companies" *Urban Studies* **10** 387–395
Galbraith J K, 1974 *Economics and the Public Purpose* (André Deutsch, London)
George K D, Silberston A, 1975 "The causes and effects of mergers" *Scottish Journal of Political Economy* **XXII** (2) 179–193
Hymer S, Rowthorn R, 1970 "Multi-national corporations and international oligopoly: the non-American challenge" in *The International Corporation* Ed C P Kindleberger (MIT Press, Cambridge, Mass.) pp 88, 90
Interplay, 1968 "Editorial—the multinational corporation: the splendours and miseries of bigness" *Interplay* November, 1–38
Nichol T, 1975 "The socialism of management: some comments on the new 'human relations'" *The Sociological Review* **23** (2)
Parsons G F, 1971 "The giant manufacturing corporations and balanced regional growth in Britain" OP, University College London
Scherer F M, 1971 *Industrial Market Structure and Economic Performance* (Rand McNally, Chicago)
Steuer M D, 1971 "Competition and the multi-national firm: the UK case" in *International Conference on Monopolies, Mergers and Restrictive Practices* Ed. J B Heath (HMSO, London) pp 211–220
Steuer M D, Abell P, Gennard J, Perlman M, Rees R, Scott B, Wallis K, 1973 *The Impact of Foreign Direct Investment on the United Kingdon* (HMSO, London)
TUC, 1974 *Industrial Democracy* report by the TUC General Council to the 1974 Trades Union Congress, July (Trades Union Congress, London)
Walshe G, 1974 *Recent Trends in Monopoly in Great Britain* (Cambridge University Press, London)

An Impact Analysis of Environmental Attraction Profiles and Spatial Mobility

P.NIJKAMP
Free University, Amsterdam

1 Introduction

The postwar period has been increasingly characterized by environmental problems. Societal priorities for material welfare and the increased land-use requirements have led to unfavourable living conditions in the industrialized part of the world. The quality of the *supply* of environmental commodities has undergone a considerable decline. In addition the *demand* structure of environmental commodities has been changed because the rise in income has led to more attention being paid to environmental commodities, so much so that they are increasingly considered as normal elements in a consumption pattern.

This poses the following question: what sort of human behaviour may be expected if the quality of the environment is not commensurate with man's preferences for environmental commodities? In principle a variety of mechanisms of social choice might be possible: for example, different attitudes with respect to the prevailing industrial technology and the present consumption pattern, the socioeconomic order, the spatial dispersion of human activities, and so forth.

In this paper, attention will be focused on the effect of environmental quality at a local or regional scale upon changes in the spatial pattern of human activities. In particular, the analysis will concentrate on the consequences of the (changed) environmental structure for *spatial mobility*. Several aspects of spatial mobility will be studied in more detail, namely behaviour with respect to migration, tourism, and commuting.

An important analytical tool, known as an *environmental profile*, will be developed in this paper. Such a profile can be conceived of as a quantitative representation of the elements of the environmental attraction of a certain place or region. By means of quantitative data on these profiles an impact analysis will be developed to investigate the degree to which environmental profiles affect man's spatial mobility. The analysis will be illustrated by a set of empirical applications for the Netherlands, and will be followed by a brief outline of possible future research.

Finally, an attempt will be made to integrate the foregoing impact analysis into a dynamic interregional model, based on a multipurpose approach for a physical planning framework. In this section particular attention will be paid to multiple-criteria decision strategies.

2 Environmental attraction profiles

A necessary condition for a quantitative approach to environmental attractiveness is the definition of the relevant environmental elements[1] in such a way that they are appropriate for an operational analysis. This requires that environmental elements should be so measured that they are comparable for different spatial points (or regions). An operational analysis of environmental elements can be obtained by introducing the idea of an *environmental profile*, which is a vector representation of the quantitative characteristics of the environmental quality at a certain place. The elements of the environmental profile of a certain place include a variety of factors: average quantity of natural areas, recreation facilities, pollution, congestion, medical care, noise, public facilities, and so on. Such an environmental profile can be determined for each place; that for a place i can be represented as:

$$\boldsymbol{p}_i = \begin{bmatrix} p_{i1} \\ \cdot \\ \cdot \\ \cdot \\ \cdot \\ p_{iJ} \end{bmatrix} = \begin{bmatrix} \text{average quantity of natural areas} \\ \text{average quantity of recreation facilities} \\ \text{degree of pollution} \\ \text{degree of annoyance} \\ \text{degree of congestion} \\ \cdot \end{bmatrix} . \qquad (1)$$

An environmental profile contains detailed information about the environmental state of a certain place in such a way that a comparison among profiles is possible. All elements p_{ij} ($j = 1, ..., J$) of the environmental profile, $\boldsymbol{p}_i$, can be measured either as cardinal or as ordinal variables, so that, for example, indices for the quality of life are also permitted. Some applications of the measures of a socioeconomic quality of life and an urban quality of life are contained in Drewnowski (1974), and House (1974). Examples of applications of such a profile analysis to ecological systems can be found in Helliwell (1969; 1974), Hooper (1971), and McHarg (1969).

The environmental profile set out above is essentially a *supply* profile: it represents a variety of environmental elements provided by the place or region in question.

The question now arises: how can one use environmental profiles as an analytical tool for studying spatial mobility? The latter may relate to several phenomena: migration, tourism, recreation, commuting, etc., so an analysis of these separate phenomena requires the use of an explanatory environmental profile containing elements closely related to the specific phenomenon. Hence the criteria for an environmental attraction profile of spatial flows are codetermined by the nature of the flows and hence are prespecified on *a priori* theoretical grounds. The foregoing multiple-

[1] Environmental elements are a broad concept covering all factors in man's physical environment that are (directly or indirectly) affected by his choice of behaviour and that, in turn, influence his choice of behaviour or his satisfaction level.

criteria representation of environmental conditions at a certain place can also be extended to the *demand* side, since each decision unit h (for example, a household) can specify a desired environmental demand profile p_h. Each element p_{hj} of p_h indicates the degree to which the availability of a certain environmental element j is demanded.

One may hypothesize that each household will attempt to realize its prespecified environmental demand profile, given its available income. By comparing the demand profile of a certain household with a series of supply profiles at different locations, an indicator for the relative environmental discrepancy of each location can be derived. This indicator can be considered as a measure of the relative quality-of-life dissatisfaction of the household in question, since the deviation between demand and supply represents the degree to which certain environmental preferences are not satisfied. The relative discrepancy between a demand profile p_h and a supply profile p_i can be measured by means of a generalized distance approach. The Euclidean distance d_{hi} between two sets p_h and p_i can be represented as follows (cf Nijkamp and Paelinck, 1975; Stone, 1960):

$$d_{hi} = [(p_h - p_i) \cdot (p_h - p_i)]^{\frac{1}{2}} . \qquad (2)$$

A necessary condition for avoiding dimensional problems in calculating the distance measure is to normalize all criteria elements of the demand and supply profiles. Instead of a Euclidean measure one could also use a more general Minkowski metric [2], m_{hi}:

$$m_{hi} = \left(\sum_{j=1}^{J} |p_{hj} - p_{ij}|^\lambda \right)^{1/\lambda} , \qquad (3)$$

where λ is a parameter of closeness which satisfies the condition $\lambda > 1$. These distance measures can be used to compare the environmental attraction differences between different locations. Clearly, a close correspondence between an environmental demand profile and an environmental supply profile will lead to a relatively low value of d_{hi} and m_{hi}. The analysis of affinities between sets of elements is a major subject in *numerical taxonomy* (see, among others, Chevalier, 1971; Guigou, 1971; Nijkamp and Paelinck, 1975; Roux, 1968; Sokal and Sneath, 1963). Numerical taxonomy attempts to identify the numerical or quantitative (dis)similarities between distinct sets. Instead of a distance measure a *similarity* measure is frequently used to quantify the degree of affinity between sets. A simple relationship between a similarity index σ_{hi} and a distance index d_{hi} (or m_{hi}) is

$$\sigma_{hi} = \frac{1}{1 + d_{hi}} . \qquad (4)$$

It can be easily seen that σ_{hi} falls between 0 and 1 as d_{hi} moves from ∞ to 0.

[2] An application of the use of Minkowski measures to regional income inequalities is contained in Bartels and Nijkamp (1976).

Instead of a similarity analysis, a more advanced technique such as *correspondence analysis* could be employed (cf Benzécri, 1973). Correspondence analysis is a specific application of pattern-recognition techniques in which relative discrepancies between different sets can be identified by means of generalized principal-component techniques. The use of these environmental profiles may also be relevant to environmental administration. By specifying a normative (or desired) environmental profile for separate places, more insight into the public-resource allocation that is required to enhance the environmental quality of different places is obtained. In the following sections a set of numerical applications of environmental profile analyses are presented.

3 An environmental impact analysis for migration

In this section an attempt is made to identify the impact of environmental profiles on migration flows, and an application to the Netherlands is presented. For many decades the western (industrialized and urbanized) part of the Netherlands has been characterized by high immigration rates. This process has only recently changed, so that at the moment the western part has a negative migration surplus. Is the change in environmental attitudes responsible for this change in the migration pattern? More precisely: do the different environmental profiles of Dutch regions offer an explanation for the interregional migration pattern, and can a shift be observed in the degree to which environmental profiles explain migration rates?

The analysis is based on aggregate interregional migration data rather than on individual migration motives. [Examples of analyses of individual migration motives of households can be found in, among others, Lave et al (1974), Lengkeek (1975), and van Naelten (1975).] In addition to environmental conditions, socioeconomic variables such as employment and income should also be taken into account (see, for example, Cebula and Vedder, 1973; Cordey-Hayes and Gleave, 1974; Klaassen and Drewe, 1973; Nijkamp, 1974a; Rogers, 1967; Somermeyer, 1971; Willis, 1972; 1974).

In general, migration decisions result from an assessment of the relative importance of push-pull factors in regions of origin and destination, respectively, together with the frictional effect of distance between regions. These push-pull factors are assumed to result from two sources, namely, *environmental* and *socioeconomic* factors, and the environmental and socioeconomic differences between regions can be measured by means of the distance concept described above. It should be noted that regional spillover effects may play a role in migration analysis since the decision to migrate to a certain region may be codetermined by positive attraction factors in surrounding regions. For example, a high demand for labour in region 1 may attract potential migrants, whereas the more attractive environment of a contiguous region 2 will induce a migration movement to the latter region (leading to commuting flows between regions 1 and 2).

Given the foregoing notions, the following formal migration model may be assumed:

$$n^m_{ii',t} = f(\Delta^s_{ii',t-1}, \Delta^e_{ii',t-1}, d_{ii'}) , \tag{5}$$

where

$n^m_{ii'}$ is the volume of migration flow from region i to i' ($i,i' = 1, ..., I$; $i \neq i'$),

$\Delta^s_{ii'}$ is the socioeconomic discrepancy between socioeconomic indicators of region i and i',

$\Delta^e_{ii'}$ is the environmental discrepancy between the environmental profile of region i and i' [cf equation (2)],

$d_{ii'}$ is the physical distance between the capital cities of region i and i', and

t is the index for the time period.

The indices t and $t-1$ indicate that migration flows in a certain period are mainly determined by a set of explanatory factors from a previous period (for a dynamic migration model, see Blokland and Nijkamp, 1974). The question now arises whether the relative importance of environmental factors can be inferred from an estimation of model (5).

The previous model was estimated on the basis of interprovincial migration data for the Netherlands. The analysis was carried out for two different periods (namely, $t = 1966$ and $t = 1972$) to determine whether the increased attention paid to environmental factors in recent years has meant that environmental discrepancies between regions have become the more important migration stimuli.

The provincial environmental profiles used in the analysis consisted largely of measures of the provision of natural areas and the recreation facilities in each province, whereas the socioeconomic indicators were represented by the differences between demand and supply of all labour categories in the province of destination. The results of the regression analysis of model (5) are presented in table 1.

Table 1. Regression results of the migration model[a].

t	Intercept	Parameter of $\Delta^s_{ii'}$	Parameter of $\Delta^e_{ii'}$	Parameter of $d_{ii'}$
1966	4962·50	0·15	715·30	−20·77
	(483·12)	(0·03)	(317·07)	(2·77)
	(10·27)	(5·03)	(1·92)	(7·48)
1972	6109·30	0·19	948·81	−23·77
	(539·62)	(0·05)	(429·83)	(3·23)
	(11·37)	(3·43)	(2·21)	(7·36)

[a] Figures in brackets represent, respectively, the standard errors of estimation and the Student t values of the corresponding parameter estimates.

The results appear to correspond with *a priori* theoretical expectations with respect to the positive and negative signs of the parameters. If one assumes a 95% confidence interval for the parameter estimates, parameter values differ significantly from zero, except the parameter associated with environmental factors in 1966 (the Student t value here is smaller than 2). This result implies that environmental quality factors cannot entirely be regarded as a significant explanatory element for migration flows during the period 1965–1966, although the F statistic indicated that the overall regression was certainly significant. The results of later periods, however, show that environmental quality factors have become the more important migration stimuli, since for the period 1971–1972 the parameter estimate associated with $\Delta_{ii'}^{e}$ is completely significant at a 95% confidence interval, a result that can also be obtained by an analysis of variance. As the migration pattern of later years is similar to that of 1971–1972, it can be concluded that environmental discrepancies among regions appear to be exerting an increasing influence upon migration flows in the Netherlands.

It should be noted that the previous model does not aim to give a complete explanation for the interprovincial migration pattern. Many other elements such as the sociocultural structure of regions might also be relevant. The attraction forces of regions appear to be composed of many heterogeneous elements. In principle, however, it is possible to calculate the implicit attractiveness of each region as it is revealed by migration flows to that region. Such a hypothesis of revealed preference can be operationalized by assuming the following gravity model for collective migration behaviour (cf Nijkamp, 1975a):

$$n_{ii'}^{m} = \alpha_{i'}^{m} d_{ii'}^{-\beta_{i'}} , \tag{6}$$

where
$\alpha_{i'}$ represents the average attractiveness of all socioeconomic, cultural, and environmental factors of region i', and
$\beta_{i'}$ is an average distance friction parameter with respect to region i' [3].
Given a set of observations on $n_{ii'}^{m}$ and $d_{ii'}$, the implicit value of $\alpha_{i'}^{m}$ and $\beta_{i'}$ can be derived by means of a log–linear regression for equation (6). The results for the eleven Dutch provinces are presented in table 2.

The results in table 2 indicate that the attractiveness parameter α_{i}^{m} is positively correlated with the distance-friction parameter, $\beta_{i'}$. These results imply that a high regional attractiveness is, in general, offset by a high distance friction (which is indeed the case for provinces like Zeeland and Limburg).

On the basis of the foregoing environmental impact analysis it can be concluded that collective migration decisions react upon environmental quality factors, therefore these factors are appropriate elements in models

---

[3] Cesario (1973) adopted a similar model to obtain implicit relative evaluations of outdoor recreation facilities (based on visits to these facilities).

that explain residential location and migration patterns. Since, in the long run, public investments in the environmental sector (creation of parks, recreation facilities, pollution abatement investments, and so forth) modify the regional environmental profiles, these investments can be considered as one of the long-term instruments that influence the pattern of residential location and the interregional migration patterns (cf section 6). The same reasoning holds true for urban–suburban movements (cf Nijkamp, 1975b). The control of these flows will only be possible if a considerable effort is made in the public sector to improve the quality of the urban environment.

Table 2. Regression results of the migration attraction model (1972)[a].

	Groningen	Friesland	Drente	Overijssel	Gelderland	Utrecht
α_i^m	12·41	14·49	13·56	15·13	13·33	15·91
	(1·72)	(2·48)	(1·97)	(2·36)	(2·86)	(1·33)
$\beta_{i'}$	1·10	1·56	1·39	1·65	1·12	1·82
	(0·34)	(0·49)	(0·39)	(0·50)	(0·61)	(0·28)

	Noord Holland	Zuid Holland	Zeeland	Noord-Brabant	Limburg
α_i^m	14·32	15·42	24·51	16·77	25·19
	(1·24)	(1·34)	(2·91)	(2·70)	(4·62)
$\beta_{i'}$	1·37	1·51	3·45	1·90	3·49
	(0·26)	(0·27)	(0·54)	(0·56)	(0·86)

[a] Figures in brackets represent standard errors of estimation.

4 An environmental impact analysis for tourism

The tourist sector is becoming progressively more important because of the growth in prosperity, the increase in the amount of leisure time, and a greater degree of mobility (and with this, the increased accessibility of many regions and countries). The provision of tourist accommodation has increased, while at the same time, in many industrialized and urbanized areas, the quality of the environment has declined (cf Bryden, 1973; Burkart and Medlik, 1974; Burton, 1970; and Clawson and Knetsch, 1966).

One way of studying tourist behaviour is to make a distinction between tourist *supply* elements and tourist *demand* elements. Supply elements are tourist-attraction forces in the region of destination, such as the quantity of natural areas, the degree of environmental attractiveness, the volume and types of holiday accommodation, the differential price levels, and so on. Demand elements are formed by the priorities for certain types of tourist facilities and accommodation, the travel time to tourist areas, family characteristics, etc.

   The subject matter of this section is again the analysis of the impacts exerted by regional environmental characteristics upon regional tourist flows. In accordance with the environmental-profile approach set out above, a reasonable method would be to construct an *environmental tourist profile* for each region separately and then to identify the influence of the profile on regional tourist flows (cf Nijkamp, 1974b). This tourist profile would include such elements as regional accessibility, availability of natural areas, quantity of recreation facilities, tourist accommodation, and cultural assets such as museums.

   Next the influence of the successive environmental attraction profiles on regional tourist flows would have to be assessed. It would be assumed that the level of tourist flows per region is a function of the tourist-attraction elements in the environmental profile, that is,

$$n_i^t = \gamma \alpha_i^t + \delta , \tag{7}$$

where

n_i^t represents total tourist flows to region i, and

α_i^t is the average tourist attractiveness of region i.

The unknown parameters γ and δ can be estimated if data on n_i^t and α_i^t are available. Obviously a serious problem is how to measure α_i^t. A simple approach would be to assign scores to all elements of the tourist profile on the basis of their relative availability or presence in the region concerned. The average score of the tourist profile can be conceived as an indicator of regional tourist attractiveness[4].

   After this, the problem of regional spillovers should be taken into account, since the volume of tourist flows to a given region is codetermined by the tourist attractiveness of surrounding regions. This implies essentially that the total attractiveness α_i^t of region i is composed of the *internal* attractiveness of region i (denoted by α_i^{ti}) and the *external* attractiveness (denoted by α_i^{tx}).

   This implies that

$$\alpha_i^t = \gamma_1 \alpha_i^{ti} + \gamma_2 \alpha_i^{tx} , \tag{8}$$

so that equation (7) can be rewritten as

$$n_i^t = \gamma_1^* \alpha_i^{ti} + \gamma_2^* \alpha_i^{tx} + \delta . \tag{9}$$

The external attractiveness α_i^{tx} of region i is defined as the weighted average (internal) attractiveness of all regions i_a contiguous to i, thus

$$\alpha_i^{tx} = \sum_{i_a} w_{i_a} \alpha_{i_a}^{ti} , \tag{10}$$

---

[4] Instead of one overall average score one could also calculate the average score for certain homogeneous subparts of the tourist profile (for example, the average natural attractiveness, the average cultural attractiveness, etc). This procedure would lead to a subdivision of α_i^t into a number of differential attractiveness indices.

where the weights w_{i_a} are formed for the successive sizes of the regions corrected for a distance friction, that is,

$$w_{i_a} = \frac{s_{i_a} \exp(-\beta d_{ii_a})}{\sum\limits_{i_a'} s_{i_a'} \exp(-\beta d_{ii_a'})} ,$$ (11)

where s_{i_a} represents the size of region i_a (contiguous to region i), and d_{ii_a} is the distance between these regions.

Substituting equation (10) into equation (8) gives

$$\alpha_i^t = \gamma_1 \alpha_i^{ti} + \gamma_2 \sum\limits_{i_a} w_{i_a} \alpha_{i_a}^{ti} ,$$ (12)

or in vector representation

$$\boldsymbol{\alpha}^t = \hat{\boldsymbol{\gamma}}_1 \boldsymbol{\alpha}^{ti} + \hat{\boldsymbol{\gamma}}_2 \mathbf{W} \boldsymbol{\alpha}^{ti} ,$$ (13)

where
$\boldsymbol{\alpha}^t$ and $\boldsymbol{\alpha}^{ti}$ are vectors in which α_i^t and α_i^{ti} are typical elements,
$\hat{\boldsymbol{\gamma}}_1$ and $\hat{\boldsymbol{\gamma}}_2$ are diagonal matrices in which γ_1 and γ_2 are main diagonal elements, and
$\mathbf{W}$ is a first-order contiguity matrix in which w_{i_a} are typical elements.
The total attractiveness can now be calculated simply as

$$\boldsymbol{\alpha}^t = (\hat{\boldsymbol{\gamma}}_1 + \hat{\boldsymbol{\gamma}}_2 \mathbf{W}) \boldsymbol{\alpha}^{ti} .$$ (14)

If, instead of equation (10), the external attractiveness α_i^{tx} of region i were to be defined as

$$\alpha_i^{tx} = \sum\limits_{i_a} w_{i_a} \alpha_{i_a}^t ,$$ (15)

then one could replace equation (13) by

$$\boldsymbol{\alpha}^t = \hat{\boldsymbol{\gamma}}_1 \boldsymbol{\alpha}^{ti} + \hat{\boldsymbol{\gamma}}_2 \mathbf{W} \boldsymbol{\alpha}^t ,$$ (16)

or

$$\boldsymbol{\alpha}^t = (\mathbf{I} - \hat{\boldsymbol{\gamma}}_2 \mathbf{W})^{-1} \hat{\boldsymbol{\gamma}}_1 \boldsymbol{\alpha}^{ti} ,$$ (17)

provided matrix $\mathbf{I} - \hat{\boldsymbol{\gamma}}_2 \mathbf{W}$ is nonsingular. The matrix $(\mathbf{I} - \hat{\boldsymbol{\gamma}}_2 \mathbf{W})^{-1}$ can be conceived as a multiplier matrix which calculates the direct and indirect attractiveness of each region, given the contiguity relationships. Equation (16) is essentially a *spatial*-autocorrelation problem (cf Cliff and Ord, 1973; Fisher, 1971; and Hordijk, 1974).

So far, the supply of tourist accommodation has been dealt with rather superficially, as one of the elements of the regional tourist profile. On the other hand it is clear that the volume of tourist flows to a certain region is limited by the tourist accommodation (hotels, camping sites, etc) in that region. In order to avoid a direct correlation between the volume of regional tourist flows and the regional tourist capacity in equation (9), the tourist flows will be measured in terms of the average regional occupation rate, r_i, of tourist accommodation, that is,

$$r_i = \frac{n_i^t}{c_i^t} , \tag{18}$$

where c_i^t represents the total tourist capacity of region i. In general, a distinction between different types l ($l = 1, ..., L$) of tourist accommodation can be made (hotels, camping sites, boarding houses, etc), so that equation (18) can be specified for each category of accommodation, thus

$$r_i^{(l)} = \frac{n_i^{t(l)}}{c_i^{t(l)}} . \tag{19}$$

Therefore, the final equation to be estimated is

$$r_i^{(l)} = \gamma_1^{(l)} \alpha_i^{ti(l)} + \gamma_2^{(l)} \alpha_i^{tx(l)} + \delta^{(l)} , \tag{20}$$

where the index (l) refers to the lth type of accommodation.

This equation has been estimated on the basis of tourist data for 1971 from fourteen tourist areas in the Netherlands. Here, instead of weights w_{i_a} [see equation (11)], an unweighted average attractiveness of contiguous regions has been used. A cross-section analysis was carried out to estimate the parameters of this equation, and the results for foreign tourists using hotel accommodation are presented in table 3.

The results show that the attractiveness of surrounding regions (that is, the external attractiveness) exerts a negative influence upon the tourism to the central region: this effect appears to be of a competitive nature. The value of the intercept is not highly statistically significant owing to the large variation in regional occupation rates.

The tourist-impact model just described enables one to analyse and project interregional tourist behaviour for all types of tourism. If the average regional tourist flows for several types of accommodation are used, the tourist effects on the regional economy can also be calculated, namely, by using a sectoral regional input–output model. In its simple form this model can be represented as

$$q_i = (\mathbf{I} - \mathbf{A}_i)^{-1} \mathbf{\Phi}_i \tag{21}$$

where

q is a vector of sectoral regional production levels,
$\mathbf{\Phi}_i$ is the final demand vector of region i, and
$(\mathbf{I} - \mathbf{A}_i)^{-1}$ represents the well-known Leontief multiplier matrix.

Table 3. Regression results for a tourist-attraction model.

$\gamma_1^{(l)}$	$\gamma_2^{(l)}$	$\delta^{(l)}$
2·68	−2·18	23·19
(0·64)	(0·77)	(15·95)

Given data on final demand, the resulting structure of regional production
can be calculated, as well as the total regional value added. The tourist
impact on the regional economy can be determined by calculating the
separate sectoral elements of the final-demand vector associated with
tourist expenditure. If each tourist category l possesses a typical
expenditure pattern, the total tourist expenditure per sector k ($k = 1, ..., K$)
in region i (denoted by $\Phi_i^{(k)}$) can be calculated as (cf Tideman, 1975):

$$\Phi_i^{(k)} = \sum_{l=1}^{L} \Phi_i^{(l,k)} = \sum_{l=1}^{L} \phi^{(l,k)} n_i^{t(l)} , \tag{22}$$

where $\Phi_i^{(l,k)}$ and $\phi^{(l,k)}$ represent the total and the average final expenditure
by tourist category l to sector k in region i, respectively. Substitution of
equation (22) into equation (21) gives the regional-production impacts of
tourism. This means that regional tourist income can be calculated as an
indirect function of the regional attractiveness. An application of the
latter input–output analysis to Drente, a tourist area in the Netherlands,
is contained in Nijkamp (1974b).

5 An environmental impact analysis for commuting
As city dwellers have become increasingly dissatisfied with the general
quality of the urban environment, large numbers of them have moved
out of the city. This movement was able to take place because higher
levels of personal prosperity meant that people could place greater priority
on a pleasant environment. Thus the process of suburbanization (and the
resulting commuting flows) can be regarded as strongly associated with
problems of urban environmental quality (cf Berry and Horton, 1974).
    The following factors are *chiefly* responsible for the large-scale process
of suburbanization:
(1) the attractiveness of a higher environmental quality in suburban areas;
(2) the occurrence of congestion and pollution in densely populated urban
    areas;
(3) the low quality and the shortage of dwellings in older urban areas
    (particularly in the postwar period);
(4) the desire to benefit from the agglomeration advantages of urban
    centres (a highly qualified service centre, shopping facilities, the
    availability of a large labour market, etc) against relatively low travel
    costs.
Commuting behaviour can be seen as the result of two opposing forces:
on the one hand, the social, cultural, and labour attractiveness of the city
centre; and on the other, the environmental and residential attractiveness
of the suburbs. Thus an analysis of commuting behaviour might start
from one of two alternative standpoints. First, for a relevant decision
unit the location of the labour market (in a built-up area) might be
assumed as given, so that the decision to commute merely leads to the
choice of a new residential location somewhere outside the built-up area.

Second, the residential location might be assumed as given, so that the decision unit then has to choose the location of the labour market. Obviously, both aspects can be integrated into one explanatory model in a stepwise way. Such a two-stage commuting analysis was carried out for the subareas of the province of Noord-Holland in the Netherlands. First, the decision to migrate from the built-up area, Amsterdam, to surrounding areas was analysed by means of the profile analysis set out in section 3. In this analysis particular attention was paid to the environmental attraction profiles of the residential areas around Amsterdam. Since this analysis is similar to that described in section 3, it will not be considered any further.

The next stage is to analyse the spatial pattern of journey-to-work decisions from the residential areas i ($i = 1, ..., I$) to Amsterdam, A. The following model was used:

$$n_{iA}^c = f(\alpha_{iA}^E, \alpha_{i_a}^E, d_{iA})$$
(23)

where

n_{iA}^c is the volume of commuters from region i to A,
α_{iA}^E is the relative labour attractiveness of region A with respect to i,
$\alpha_{i_a}^E$ is the relative labour attractiveness of contiguous regions i_a of region i, and
d_{iA} is the distance between region i and A.

The results of the regression analysis are represented in table 4 [5].

The next section is devoted to an integration and extension of the previous types of analysis.

Table 4. Regression results of the commuting model.

Intercept	Parameter of α_{iA}^E	Parameter of $\alpha_{i_a}^E$	Parameter of d_{iA}
3·60	2·44	−0·31	−0·06
(0·43)	(0·59)	(0·13)	(0·01)

6 Extensions of the analysis

In previous sections several aspects of spatial *processes* (migration, tourism, commuting) were analysed. It was suggested that a variety of elements from the spatial *structure* could be identified as explanatory factors for these spatial processes. Next, the question arises as to whether the total pattern of spatial processes can be integrated with the various regional profiles that characterize the spatial structure.

This implies, from a formal point of view, that one set of elements (namely, the flow variables) should be related to the other set of elements (the items forming a regional profile), and statistically this would require

[5] The author is indebted to F W Schreuder who carried out this analysis.

an application of *canonical correlation*. Canonical correlation is a statistical technique which attempts to explain a multiplicity of criteria by a multiplicity of underlying factors (cf Anderson, 1958), thus providing a description of the relationships and correlations between two *sets* of phenomena.

A serious problem in the use of canonical correlation is the fact that the elements of the two sets are frequently not linearly independent. This problem of multicollinearity can be avoided by applying principal-component analysis to each set separately and by using component scores as input data for the canonical analysis.

Canonical-correlation analysis is useful for identifying the relative contribution of the elements of spatial structure to the occurrence of various spatial processes, and applications of the technique to problems of regional income and regional migration rates are found in Bartels and Nijkamp (1976) and Willis (1972), respectively.

Another extension of the foregoing spatial-profile analysis would be to use a *spectral analysis* both for the elements of the spatial profile and for the elements of the spatial flow processes. This would require the construction of cross-section, Fourier wave-like functions (see, among others, Fishman, 1969; Granger and Hatanaka, 1965; and Rayner, 1971). A mutual comparison of the separate Fourier functions associated with the successive elements might shed more light on the affinities between profile elements and flow elements. The degree to which spectral analysis can be integrated with canonical correlation analysis might be worth further attention. Applications of spectral analysis in a spatial context are contained in Bassett and Haggett (1971), Granger (1969), Moellering and Tobler (1972), and Rayner and Golledge (1972).

7 A dynamic multiple-criteria profile model

In previous sections the idea of a regional profile was introduced as a means of examining the factors underlying spatial mobility. The analysis presented so far has been mainly static and has not included aspects of spatial policy for controlling mobility. In this final section a model, which can be regarded as a formal policy-control model for spatial mobility, will be developed by taking into account regional environmental profiles and regional interactions.

The crucial relationship for spatial mobility of a certain type, k, (migration, recreation, tourism, commuting, etc) is

$$\dot{n}^k = f^k(n^k, p^e, p_a^e, p^s, p_a^s, d) , \tag{24}$$

where
n^k is a vector of flows of type k to region i (with typical elements n_i^k; $i = 1, ..., I$);
$\dot{n}^k$ is the time derivative of n^k;
f^k is a vector-valued function;

p^e is the environmental profile of region i (with typical elements p_i^e; $i = 1, ..., I$);

p_a^e is the environmental profile of contiguous regions of region i (with typical elements $p_{i_a}^e$);

p^s is the socioeconomic profile (production, income, employment, etc) of region i (with typical elements p_i^s; $i = 1, ..., I$);

p_a^s is the socioeconomic profile of contiguous regions of region i (with typical elements $p_{i_a}^s$);

d is the distance vector for all separate regions [with average distance d_i $(i = 1, ..., I)$ as typical elements].

This dynamic-profile model includes a basic element of spatial mobility, namely, *external spillover* effects. The flows to a certain region are codetermined by the environmental and socioeconomic profiles of surrounding regions (as was demonstrated in the profile models of earlier sections of this paper). In addition the time-varying changes $\dot{n}^k$ are also codetermined by the states n^k of these variables in a previous period. There are two reasons for this specification. First, there is frequently a considerable (lagged) imitation in human behaviour, so that a choice in favour of a certain decision is adopted by other people in a following period. Second, the volume of a flow to a certain region may reach a particular threshold level, so that beyond this threshold level the region is no longer attractive for new people. This is a well-known phenomenon in traffic studies (for example, congestion; and in recreation studies, namely, recreational capacities; cf Stankey, 1972).

If one assumes that this dynamic impact model can be specified or approximated by means of a linear model, the following result is obtained:

$$\dot{n}^k = A_1^k n^k + A_2^k p^e + A_3^k p_a^e + A_4^k p^s + A_5^k p_a^s + A_6^k d . \tag{25}$$

The next stage to be considered is the influence of exogenous variables upon the various regional profiles. The following impact model may be assumed:

$$\dot{p}^e = f(p^e, i^e, i^s) , \tag{26}$$

where i^e and i^s represent regional vectors of investments in the environmental sector (pollution abatement investments, construction of parks and recreational facilities, etc) and in the socioeconomic sector (private investments, social-overhead investments, etc). The socioeconomic profile can be dealt with in a similar way, thus

$$\dot{p}^s = f(p^s, i^e, i^s) . \tag{27}$$

If, instead of the last two general impact models, a linear specification is assumed, the result becomes

$$\dot{p}^e = B_1 p^e + B_2 i^e + B_3 i^s , \tag{28}$$

and

$$\dot{p}^s = C_1 p^s + C_2 i^e + C_3 i^s .$$ (29)

The above models form a description of the relationships between spatial mobility, spatial profiles, and regional-investment decisions. An important characteristic of these types of models is the fact that ultimately the spatial flows to a certain region are a function of the (environmental and socioeconomic) investments in surrounding regions. It is obvious that this phenomenon necessitates a spatial coordination and harmonization of environmental policies (cf Alessio, 1972). For economic and policy reasons the free movement of such a spatial interdependent system is frequently rather limited. First, one should take account of the available investment budget in each period, that is

$$i^e + i^s \leqslant i^R ,$$ (30)

where i^R represents the regional investment budget. If, instead of a separate investment budget in each region, a national-investment budget is assumed (as in a pooling model), the following investment condition is relevant:

$$1'i^e + 1'i^s \leqslant i^N ,$$ (31)

where 1 represents a vector with unit elements (a summation vector) and i^N the national investment budget.

Next it is reasonable to specify critical minimum values for the regional environmental profiles:

$$p^e \geqslant p^{Re} .$$ (32)

In a similar way one may impose a feasible area for the successive regional flows

$$\check{n}^{R,k} \leqslant n^{R,k} \leqslant \hat{n}^{R,k} ,$$ (33)

where $\check{n}^{R,k}$ and $\hat{n}^{R,k}$ represent minimum and maximum regional flows of type k, respectively.

The use of the previous dynamic model as a policy-control model (or planning model) for an adequate spatial dispersion of human activities requires the specification of a social objective function. Given the nature of the foregoing structural model, and given recent discussions about policy objectives in this field, two objectives will be taken into account.

First, each region should have a socioeconomic structure such that total *long-term social benefits* are at a maximum. This leads to the following objective function W_1:

$$\max W_1 = \int_0^T \exp(-rt) f^s(i^s) \, dt ,$$ (34)

where r is the rate of discount and f^s a scalar-valued function which transforms the investment vector i^s into national net benefits. A linear specification of this objective function would give the following result:

$$\max W_1^* = \int_0^T \exp(-rt)\pi \cdot i^s \, dt \,, \tag{35}$$

where π represents a vector of net social benefits accruing from a unit of investment.

A second social objective may be the *preservation or even extension of the environmental quality* of each region. This would imply the following objective function W_2:

$$\max W_2 = \int_0^T \exp(-rt)f^e(p^e) \, dt \,, \tag{36}$$

where f^e is a scalar-valued function which transforms the elements of the environmental profiles into relevant environmental quality characteristics (like ecological stability and ecological variety). Maximization of these environmental indicators is becoming an increasingly important objective in physical planning. If this function can be approximated in a linear way, one obtains

$$\max W_2^* = \int_0^T \exp(-rt)\epsilon \cdot p^e \, dt \,, \tag{37}$$

where ϵ is an ecological quality indicator (cf Helliwell, 1969; 1974).

If either W_1 or W_2 were to be selected as a relevant unidimensional policy decision-criterion, maximization of this criterion subject to the aforementioned constraints would lead to a single-criterion optimal-control model. Applications of optimal-control theory to environmental administration are found, for example, in Fisher et al (1972), Herfindahl and Kneese (1974), Nijkamp (1974c), Nijkamp and Paelinck (1973), and Nijkamp and Verhage (1976). If the side conditions and the performance criterion include nonlinear functions, optimal-control models can be solved by means of penalty methods (cf Lasdon et al, 1967b), Newton–Raphson methods (cf Schley and Imsong Lee, 1967), gradient methods (cf Fair, 1974; and Lasdon et al, 1967a), or iterative sweep methods (cf Nijkamp, 1974c). Should all relationships be linear functions, then optimal-control problems can easily be solved as traditional, dynamic linear-programming models.

A basic problem of the decision model described above is the existence of *multiple*-decision criteria, namely, the maximization of social benefits as well as the maximization of environmental quality. Obviously the question arises as to how to reconcile these conflicting, or at least different, criteria. The existence of several decision criteria is a common phenomenon in public administration and physical planning, but the computational and methodological aspects of this problem are very hard to overcome.

Instead of evaluating the state of a system on the basis of one single performance index, attention should be focused on a decision framework with a variety of preference indicators. This problem is precisely the subject matter of *multiple-objective programming theory* (see, for example, Geoffrion, 1968; Klahr, 1958; and Zeleny and Cochrane, 1973). The salient feature of multiple-objective programming methods is the existence of a multiplicity of preference criteria $(W_1, W_2, ...)$.

From a methodological point of view, in general, a simultaneous optimization of all decision criteria will not lead to one unique optimum. The traditional solution techniques for programming models (for example, the Kuhn–Tucker theorems) are not directly applicable. Fortunately, however, a set of methods has been developed which attempts to overcome the problems caused by the multidimensionality of decision criteria (see, for example, Chang, 1966; Da Cunha and Polak, 1967; Ho, 1970; Klinger, 1964; Rao and Rajamani, 1975; Salama and Gourishankar, 1971; and Zadeh, 1963).

One way of approaching multiple-criteria programming problems is to determine one or more *efficient solutions* instead of one global optimum solution (see Zeleny, 1974). An efficient solution is one that falls into the feasible area and maximizes a certain decision criterion in such a way that its value cannot be increased without decreasing the values of other decision criteria. The decision problem is then reduced to a choice among a limited number of (at least reasonable) solutions.

A second method is to provide each decision criterion separately with a relevant *political weight* (trade-off or rate of substitution). In this case the multiple-objective programming model is reduced to a traditional programming model, provided that the original problem can be written as a weighted linear combination of the original performance criteria (see also Salama and Gourishankar, 1971).

Third, the successive preference criteria can be ranked by means of *hierarchical optimization criteria* (cf Waltz, 1967). This method is a sequential optimization technique which depends on the ranking of the preference criteria.

Another solution method for multiple-criteria problems is to use one of the decision criteria as a *dominant criterion* and to impose adequate *limits* on the values of the other decision criteria. Then the multiple-objective programming model is reduced to a traditional single-criterion programming problem.

Finally, if a choice has to be made among a limited set of alternative solutions on the basis of several decision criteria, a so-called *concordance* analysis can be applied (cf Nijkamp, 1975c; Nijkamp and van Delft, 1976). A concordance analysis attempts to evaluate alternative states of a system by seeking a dominant alternative on the basis of a set of weights for each criterion separately.

Clearly the computational complexity of large, nonlinear, optimal-control models will sometimes preclude an efficient solution (cf Schupp, 1972). Fortunately, considerable progress is being made in the field of dynamic nonlinear optimization theory. Although the multiple-objective profile model set out above is not yet in an operational stage, nevertheless it provides insight into the spatial complexity and interwovenness of public decisionmaking. Given both the aforementioned solution techniques and the necessary information, it seems reasonable to expect that the profile analysis will be an operational tool for multiple-criteria decisionmaking in the field of physical planning and environmental management.

References
Alessio F J, 1972 "Environmental quality control: social rules and economic problems" *Review of Social Economy* **30** (3) 340-351
Anderson T W, 1958 *An Introduction to Multivariate Statistical Analysis* (John Wiley, New York)
Bartels C P A, Nijkamp P, 1976 "An empirical welfare approach to regional income distributions" *Socio-Economic Planning Sciences* **10** 117-128
Bassett K, Haggett P, 1971 "Towards short-term forecasting for cyclic behaviour in a regional system of cities" in *Regional Forecasting* Eds M Chisholm, A E Frey, P Haggett (Butterworths, London) pp 319-413
Benzécri J P, 1973 *L'analyse des Données* (Dunod, Paris)
Berry B J L, Horton F E, 1974 *Urban Environmental Management* (Prentice-Hall, Englewood Cliffs, NJ)
Blokland J, Nijkamp P, 1974 "Some dynamic models for spatial interactions" *Foundations of Empirical Economic Research* Netherlands Economic Institute, Rotterdam
Bryden J M, 1973 *Tourism and Development* (Cambridge University Press, Cambridge)
Burkart A J, Medlik S, 1974 *Tourism* (Heinemann, London)
Burton T L (Ed.), 1970 *Recreation, Research and Planning* (Allen and Unwin, London)
Cebula R J, Vedder R K, 1973 "A note on migration, economic opportunity, and the quality of life" *Journal of Regional Science* **13** (2) 204-211
Cesario F J, 1973 "A generalized trip distribution model" *Journal of Regional Science* **13** (2) 233-247
Chang S S L, 1966 "General theory of optimal processes" *Journal of SIAM Control* **4** 46-55
Chevalier J C, 1971 *Classification et Régionalisation: Analyse des Méthodes Quantitatives* Ph D thesis, University of Dijon, Dijon, France
Clawson M, Knetsch J L, 1966 *The Economics of Outdoor Recreation* (Johns Hopkins University Press, Baltimore, Md)
Cliff A O, Ord J K, 1973 *Spatial Autocorrelation* (Pion, London)
Cordey-Hayes M, Gleave D, 1974 "Migration movements and the differential growth of city regions in England and Wales" *Papers of the Regional Science Association* **33** 99-123
Da Cunha N O, Polak E, 1967 "Constrained minimization under vector-valued criteria in finite dimensional spaces" *Journal of Mathematical Analysis and Applications* **19** 103-124
Drewnowski J, 1974 *On Measuring and Planning the Quality of Life* (Mouton, The Hague)
Fair R C, 1974 "Methods for computing optimal control solutions: on the solutions of optimal control problems as maximization problems" *Annals of Economic and Social Measurement* **3** (1) 135-154

Fisher A C, Krutilla J V, Cicchetti C J, 1972 "The economics of environmental preservation: a theoretical and empirical analysis" *American Economic Review* **62** 605-619

Fisher W A, 1971 "Econometric estimation with spatial dependence" *Regional and Urban Economics* **1** (1) 19-40

Fishman G, 1969 *Spectral Methods in Econometrics* (Harvard University Press, Cambridge, Mass)

Geoffrion A M, 1968 "Proper efficiency and the theory of vector maximization" *Journal of Mathematical Analysis and Applications* **22** 618-630

Granger C W J, 1969 "Spatial data and time series analysis" in *London Papers in Regional Science 1. Studies in Regional Science* Ed. A J Scott (Pion, London) pp 1-24

Granger C W J, Hatanaka M, 1965 *Spectral Analysis of Economic Time Series* (Princeton University Press, Princeton, NJ)

Guigou J L, 1971 *Analyse Economique et Analyse Multidimensionelle* (Dunod, Paris)

Helliwell D R, 1969 "Valuation of wildlife resources" *Regional Studies* **3** 41-47

Helliwell D R, 1974 "The value of vegetation for conservation" *Journal of Environmental Management* **2** 51-78

Herfindahl O C, Kneese A V, 1974 *Economic Theory of Natural Resources* (Merrill, Columbus, Ohio)

Ho Y C, 1970 "Differential games, dynamic optimization and generalized control theory" *Journal of Optimization Theory and Application* **6** (3) 179-209

Hooper M D, 1971 "The size and surroundings of nature reserves" in *The Scientific Management of Animal and Plant Communities for Conservation* Eds S J Duffey, D E Watt (Blackwell, Oxford) pp 555-561

Hordijk L, 1974 "Spatial correlation in the disturbances of a linear interregional model" *Regional and Urban Economics* **4** 117-140

House P, 1974 *The Urban Environmental System* (Sage Publications, Beverly Hills, Calif.)

Klaassen L H, Drewe P, 1973 *Migration Policy in Europe* (Saxon House, New York)

Klahr C N, 1958 "Multiple objectives in mathematical programming" *Operations Research* **6** (6) 849-855

Klinger A, 1964 "Vector-valued performance criteria" *IEEE Transactions on Automatic Control* **AC-9** 117-118

Lasdon L S, Mitter S K, Waren A D, 1967a "The conjugate gradient method for optimal control problems" *IEEE Transactions on Automatic Control* **AC-12** (2) 132-138

Lasdon L S, Waren A D, Rice R K, 1967b "An interior penalty method for inequality constrained optimal control problems" *IEEE Transactions on Automatic Control* **AC-12** (4) 388-395

Lave L B, Lave J R, Seskin E P, 1974 "Migration and urban change" in *Transport and the Urban Environment* Eds J G Rothenberg, I G Heggie (Macmillan, London) pp 99-131

Lengkeek J, 1975 "Vliegtuighinder en migratie" Geographic Institute, Free University, Amsterdam

McHarg I L, 1969 *Design with Nature* (Natural History Press, New York)

Moellering H, Tobler W, 1972 "Geographical variances" *Geographical Analysis* **4** (1) 34-50

Naelten M van, 1975 "Motivation in suburban migrations related to environmental standards: an analysis of the Antwerp regional migrations" paper presented at the Conference on Regional Science, Energy and Environment, Louvain, Belgium

Nijkamp P, 1974a "Milieu en migratie" *Economisch-Statistische Berichten* **59** (2981) 1115-1119

Nijkamp P, 1974b "Environmental attraction forces and regional tourist effects" RM-14, Department of Economics, Free University, Amsterdam

Nijkamp P, 1974c "Spatial interdependencies and environmental effects" in *Dynamic Allocation of Urban Space* Eds A Karlqvist, L Lundqvist, F Snickars (Saxon House, Teakfield, Farnborough, Hants.) pp 175-209

Nijkamp P, 1975a "Operational determination of collective preference parameters" RM-17, Department of Economics, Free University, Amsterdam

Nijkamp P, 1975b "Urbane en suburbane leefbaarheidsperikelen" in *Stedelijk Perspektief* Eds P Nijkamp, C Verhage (Stenfert Kroese, Leyden) pp 1-36

Nijkamp P, 1975c "A multi-criteria analysis for project evaluation; economic-ecological evaluation of a land reclamation project" *Papers of the Regional Science Association* **34** 87-114

Nijkamp P, Delft A van, 1976 "A multi-objective decision model for regional development, environmental quality control and industrial land use" *Papers of the Regional Science Association* **36** (forthcoming)

Nijkamp P, Paelinck J H P, 1973 "Some models for the economic evaluation of the environment" *Regional and Urban Economics* **3** (1) 33-62

Nijkamp P, Paelinck J H P, 1975 *Operational Theory and Method in Regional Economics* (Saxon House, Teakfield, Farnborough, Hants.) (forthcoming)

Nijkamp P, Verhage C, 1976 "Cost-benefit analysis and optimal control theory for environmental decisions: a case study of the Dollard Estuary" in *Environment, Regional Science and Interregional Modeling* Eds M Chatterji, P van Rompuy (Springer Verlag, Berlin) pp 74-110

Rao P K, Rajamani V S, 1975 "A new approach to public investment" *Socio-Economic Planning Sciences* **9** 11-14

Rayner J N, 1971 *Introduction to Spectral Analysis* (Pion, London)

Rayner J N, Golledge R G, 1972 "Spectral analysis of settlement patterns in diverse physical and economic environments" *Environment and Planning* **4** 347-371

Rogers A, 1967 "A regression analysis of interregional migration in California" *Review of Economics and Statistics* **49** 262-267

Roux M, 1968 *Un Algorithme pour Construire une Hiérarchie Particulière* (Thèse Sciences, Paris)

Salama A I A, Gourishankar V, 1971 "Optimal control of systems with a single control and several cost functionals" *International Journal of Control* **14** (4) 705-725

Schley C H, Imsong Lee, 1967 "Optimal control computation by the Newton-Raphson method and the Riccati transformation" *IEEE Transactions on Automatic Control* **AC-12** (2) 139-144

Schupp F R, 1972 "Uncertainty and stabilization for a nonlinear model" *Quarterly Journal of Economics* **86** 94-110

Sokal R R, Sneath P H A, 1963 *Principles of Numerical Taxonomy* (Freeman, San Francisco)

Somermeyer W H, 1971 "Multi-polar human flow models" *Papers of the Regional Science Association* **26** 131-144

Stankey G H, 1972 "A strategy for the definition and management of wilderness quality" in *Natural Environments: Studies in Theoretical and Applied Analysis* Ed. J L Krutilla (Johns Hopkins University Press, Baltimore, Md) pp 88-114

Stone J R N, 1960 "A comparison of the economic structures of regions based on the concept of distance" *Journal of Regional Science* **2** (2) 1-20

Tideman M C, 1975 *Recreatie en Economie* (Stichting Recreatie, The Hague)

Waltz F M, 1967 "An engineering approach: hierarchical optimization criteria" *IEEE Transactions on Automatic Control* **AC-12** (2) 179-180

Willis K G, 1972 "The influence of spatial structure and socio-economic factors on migration rates" *Regional Studies* **6** 69–82

Willis K G, 1974 *Problems in Migration Analysis* (Saxon House, Teakfield, Farnborough, Hants.)

Zadeh L A, 1963 "Optimality and nonscalar-valued performance criteria" *IEEE Transactions on Automatic Control* **AC-8** 59–60

Zeleny M, Cochrane J L (Eds), 1973 *Multiple Criteria Decision Making* (University of South Carolina Press, South Carolina)

Zeleny M, 1974 *Linear Multiobjective Programming* (Springer-Verlag, Berlin)

Calibrating a Disaggregated Residential Allocation Model—DRAM

S.H.PUTMAN
University of Pennsylvania

Introduction

As part of a research effort, sponsored by the National Science Foundation, to compare the performances of two different land-use models calibrated on the same data base, several fundamental problems in urban land-use modelling have been encountered and partially resolved. In particular, the fact that no Lowry-derivative, land-use model had ever been properly calibrated in work done in the US became abundantly clear. In order, then, to accomplish the desired comparison of different models on a common data base, it became necessary to develop a calibration procedure for these models. The development of this calibration procedure suggested, in turn, a reformulation of the model into one which appears to be much superior to the original and which is sufficiently different to justify a new name, Disaggregated Residential Allocation Model—DRAM, to differentiate it from its predecessor. A rather unique characteristic of this model, cast in entropy-maximizing form, is its multivariate attractiveness measure.

Background

The development of the Lowry model of land-use distribution (Lowry, 1964), along with that of numerous derivatives of its basic structure, has been described elsewhere (Goldner, 1971; Putman, 1975). Some years after development of these models had begun in the US, further substantial development of them was undertaken in Great Britain (Batty, 1972). Interestingly, despite the fact that the model originated in the US, some of the most fruitful work in extending the concept has been done in recent years in Great Britain. Further, and of critical importance to applications of the model, the question of estimation of the model's parameters has (as far as I know) never been propertly settled in any US work, with perhaps one exception, that of Voorhees and associates (1972). In contrast, it appears that the British work has produced rather conclusive evidence about the means by which these models may be calibrated (Batty, 1970; Batty and Mackie, 1972).

A modified version of the Incremental Projective Land Use Model (IPLUM) was used in the Integrated Transportation and Land Use Package (ITLUP). This ITLUP version of IPLUM is fully described elsewhere (Putman, 1973). In brief, the residential portion of this model allocates increments of residential locators to their places of residence in response to increments in basic employment and changes in the transportation facilities. This response is determined by a probability function that describes the distribution of work trips, and by a measure of residential attractiveness for each potential location zone. The purpose of this paper is to outline the steps thought to be necessary for a proper calibration of the ITLUP–IPLUM model, and which ultimately led to the development of DRAM.

Virtually all derivates of the Lowry model used in the US have, as their residential-allocation function, some form of the following expression:

$$N_i = g \sum_j p_{ij} E_j \,, \tag{1}$$

where

N_i is the number of residential locators locating in area i,
p_{ij} is the probability of living in area i and working in area j,
E_j is the number of employees in area j, and
g is a scaling factor such that the sum of the N_i over all i is equal to an exogenous control total.

There are often other scaling or multiplier factors to convert from employees to households and to ensure various types of internal consistency.

The probability p_{ij} is the most important component of equation (1). In the original Lowry model, the function used was

$$p_{ij} = (d_{ij})^{-1 \cdot 33R} \,, \tag{2}$$

where

d_{ij} is the airline distance between the centroids of area i and area j, and
R is the number of zones in an annulus d_{ij} miles from the origin.

In various derivatives of the Lowry model, p_{ij} is modified to include measures of the attractiveness of area i. In particular, in the ITLUP form of IPLUM,

$$p_{ij} = f(d_{ij})O_i \,, \tag{3}$$

where

$$f(d_{ij}) = \frac{\beta}{d_{ij}^2} \exp\left(\alpha - \frac{\beta}{d_{ij}}\right), \tag{4}$$

O_i is a measure of residential 'opportunities' in i,
d_{ij} is the travel time between centroids of zones i and j, and
α, β are empirically derived parameters.

The measure of opportunities is basically an adjusted measure of residential holding capacity (previous level of residential density times amount of available land). The adjustment, Q_i, is a logistic-curve function of the proportion of the developable land in zone i that has been developed by the end of the base time period. Thus

$$O_i = a_i^y \left(\frac{h_i}{a_i^r} \right) Q_i ,$$ (5)

where
a_i^y is the vacant acreage in zone i,
h_i is the number of housing units in zone i,
a_i^r is the residential acreage in zone i, and
Q_i is a factor that denotes the level of development.
This factor is defined as

$$Q_i = 1 - \frac{\gamma}{(1-\gamma)\exp(\delta x_i^2)} ,$$ (6)

where
γ, δ are parameters, and
x_i is the percentage of developable land area in zone i that has been
      developed.

The parameters of the trip function were estimated by fitting the
equation to observed work-trip distributions from the San Francisco area.
The parameters of the development-level function, Q_i, have not been
statistically estimated nor has the complete probability function, p_{ij}, been
fitted to any actual data. It was precisely this fitting which was necessary,
but which had never been done (with the exception of Voorhees' attempt)
in US work with derivatives of the Lowry model.

Reformulation of the model

In all of these models the essence of the residential allocations is either
the work-trip (home-to-work or work-to-home) or a combination of the
work-trip with measures of attractiveness of the potential residential
locations. Hence a set of work trips is implied when any of these models
is used to estimate residential locations, but very little use has been made
of this fact in US work. Yet, it is precisely the existence of these implicit
trip matrices that leads to a more satisfactory method of estimating the
parameters of these models. The use of IPLUM in the ITLUP package is
a particular exception to the usual practice of ignoring these implicit
trips. In this case these implicit work trips are made explicit by extracting
the trips from the model directly, and these trips are later used to load the
transport network (Putman, 1973).

It is a virtue (and perhaps, in the first instance, was the source) of the
Wilson entropy-maximizing approach to the analysis of these models that
the question of these trips is made explicit (Wilson, 1967). For example,
based on this approach (Wilson, 1970), the Lowry model may be
rewritten as

$$T_{ij} = E_j \, f(c_{ij}) ,$$ (7)

where

T_{ij} is the number of persons working in zone j and residing in zone i,

E_j is the number of persons working in zone j, and

c_{ij} is the impedence (usually travel time or travel cost) between centroids of zone i and zone j.

An important problem of this formulation is that there is no constraint on the sums of trips, in which case there is no reason to expect that

$$\sum_i T_{ij} = E_j \ . \tag{8}$$

This implies that the number of employees in zone j will not necessarily be equal to the sum of the employees residing in all zones i who claim to work in zone j.

A simple residential-location model may be derived from entropy-maximizing concepts as follows:

$$T_{ij} = A_i B_j O_i E_j \, \mathrm{f}(c_{ij}) \ , \tag{9}$$

where now

T_{ij} is the number of trips between zones i and j, or the number of persons living in zone i and working in zone j,

O_i is the number of trip origins, or the number of employed persons living in zone i,

E_j is the number of trip destinations or the number of employees employed in zone j,

A_i is a balancing factor for trip origins,

B_j is a balancing factor for trip destinations, and

c_{ij} is an impedance function.

It is possible to replace the trip origins O_i by a measure of attractiveness of the origin zone, W_i. This eliminates the need for the origins balancing factor A_i, thus giving

$$T_{ij} = B_j W_i E_j \, \mathrm{f}(c_{ij}) \ . \tag{10}$$

In order for the constraint on the sums of trip destinations, given by equation (8), to be met, we have

$$B_j = \frac{1}{\sum_i W_i \, \mathrm{f}(c_{ij})} \ . \tag{11}$$

It is informative to substitute this expression back into the original equation (Senior, 1973), this yields

$$T_{ij} = E_j \left[\frac{W_i \, \mathrm{f}(c_{ij})}{\sum_i W_i \, \mathrm{f}(c_{ij})} \right] \ . \tag{12}$$

If the term $W_i \, \mathrm{f}(c_{ij})$ is called an 'accessibility attractiveness' measure, then the fraction in equation (12) is a relative measure of the accessibility–attractiveness of zone i to zone j compared to all other zones i.

Further, it is clear that the total number of employed residents residing in zone i is

$$N_i = \sum_j T_{ij} \, , \tag{13}$$

where

$$N_i = \sum_j \left\{ E_j \left[\frac{W_i f(c_{ij})}{\sum\limits_i W_i f(c_{ij})} \right] \right\} . \tag{14}$$

If one is willing to assert that

$$p_{ij} = \frac{W_i f(c_{ij})}{\sum\limits_i W_i f(c_{ij})} \, ,$$

then equation (14) is equivalent to saying that

$$N_i = \sum_j E_j p_{ij} \, , \tag{15}$$

which is the same function as that of the Lowry model, and described in equation (1).

Thus it can be seen that the IPLUM allocation procedure may be considered, in the context of the entropy-maximizing formulation, as a simple residential-location model. However, IPLUM is a dynamic model in that it estimates changes in the number of residential locators as follows:

$$\Delta N_i = \sum_j (\Delta E_j) p_{ij} \, , \tag{16}$$

where

ΔN_i is the change in the number of employed residents of zone i from time t to time $t+1$,

ΔE_j is the change in the number of employees in zone j from time t to time $t+1$, and

p_{ij} is the probability that a person will live in zone i and work in zone j, at time $t+1$.

A question arises here as to whether Δp_{ij} might be more appropriate in the new formulation than p_{ij}. Unfortunately, the resolution of this question leads to the further question, among others, of location of in-migrants versus the location of intrametropolitan movers. In-migrants probably make their location decisions somewhat differently than the intrametropolitan movers. None of the Lowry class of models deals properly with this question. The TOMM models (Crecine, 1964; 1969) do so in a very superficial way by means of the 'stable-household' functions. It was not possible to resolve this problem in the current work, so the existing practice of using p_{ij} has been maintained for the present. Furthermore, as will be discussed below, it was the static form of the model that was finally estimated.

Calibration: initial discussion

To date, virtually all attempts in the US to calibrate these models have involved assorted procedures, no one of which achieved any more than a partial calibration of the allocation function. Some procedures have fitted $f(d_{ij})$, as in equation (2) or equation (4), to observed trip data without taking into account the effects of the characteristics of the origin zone or the destination zone. Other calibration attempts have fitted a function with N_i as the dependent variable and various characteristics of zone i as independent variables, thus ignoring any explicit consideration of the trip distribution. Neither of these two procedures nor any of their many variations is capable of estimating properly the parameters of such a model.

For a model expressed in the form of equation (9), the only parameter(s) to be estimated is that/are those which may be included in $f(c_{ij})$. It has been shown that, in fitting the parameters for such a model, statistics that summarized the goodness-of-fit of the work-trip distributions were much more sensitive to changes in model parameters than those that summarized the goodness-of-fit of the activity distributions (Batty, 1970). This result argues for the use, when possible, of work-trip statistics as criteria for model calibration. Other work has derived several types of statistics that have summarized the distributions of the work trips, each of which is appropriate for particular functional forms of $f(c_{ij})$ (Hyman, 1969).

A problem posed by the form of the model shown in equation (10) is that W_i, the attractiveness measure, is not a directly observable or measurable variable. In one attempt to model this, the number of dwellings in zone i or the population in zone i were proposed as proxy measures of W_i (Cripps and Foot, 1969). Population was finally selected and produced quite acceptable calibration results. In another attempt, usable land area in zone i was suggested as a proxy measure of W_i (Barras et al., 1971). In both of these cases, by using a single proxy variable for W_i, calibration of the model remains a matter of estimating the parameter(s) of $f(c_{ij})$.

In these cases, as well as those using the original form of the model in equation (9), the calibration process involves, (1) selecting starting values of the parameters, (2) estimating the trip distribution, (3) comparing the estimated trip distribution to the actual trip distribution, (4) revising the parameter values, and (5) iterating to find the best-fit parameter values. Work has been done on efficient means of doing this (Hyman, 1969; Batty and Mackie, 1972).

At this point, it becomes necessary to introduce a further consideration, the need to disaggregate the residential locators into types. First, we acknowledge that this disaggregation may easily be described in terms of the entropy-maximizing approach by considering T_{ij}^{kw} to be the number of employees of type w who work in zone j and live in type k housing in zone i. An appropriate set of equations and constraints can be developed to cover this situation as well as several others (Wilson, 1970). Solving such a model involves an endogenous procedure for estimating the housing stock by zone. This is not a welcome prospect for our current research efforts, though clearly it is a consideration for the future. What is necessary, then, is a model in the form of equation (10), but disaggregated only by type of locator. This may be written as

$$T_{ij}^k = B_j^k E_j W_i^k f_k(c_{ij}) ,$$ (17)

where

$$B_j^k = \left[\sum_i W_i^k f_k(c_{ij}) \right]^{-1} .$$ (18)

Second, it seemed desirable to investigate the use of a multivariate attractiveness measure. There is empirical evidence that the attractiveness of zone i is a function of, among other variables, the distribution of household types living in zone i (Putman, 1973). This evidence suggests that the attractiveness of a zone to a particular household type is a function of the percentage composition of household types in that zone. Further, the amount of developable land in a zone seems to be a determining factor in residential location, as does a developability factor which appears to act as a proxy variable for the extent of the available urban infrastructure. Thus W_i^k may be defined as follows:

$$W_i^k = \left[\sum_g a_g^k \left(\frac{N_{ig}}{\sum_g N_{ig}} \right) \right] r_i L_i^v Q_i$$ (19)

where
a_g^k are parameters to be estimated,
N_{ig} is the number of households of type g in zone i (note the g household types correspond directly to the k household types),
r_i is residential density, that is households acre^{-1} in zone i,
L_i^v is the available, developable, vacant land in zone i, and
Q_i has the same definition as in equation (6).

The parameters in the expression for Q_i may be estimated independently of the rest of the model. The parameters a_g^k need to be estimated within the structure of the model; in addition, the parameter(s) of $f_k(c_{ij})$ must also be estimated in the same way.

The precise form of the model desired would be, as in the previous discussions, dynamic rather than static, that is

$$\Delta T_{ij}^k = B_j^k W_i^k (\Delta E_j^k) f_k(c_{ij}) .$$ (20)

To do this it would be necessary to have data for ΔT_{ij}^k and ΔE_j^k. While this work was in progress these data were not available, so it was impossible to estimate any but the static model.

In order to specify data requirements it will be helpful to write out the model in full. Thus

$$T_{ijt}^k = B_j^k W_{it}^k E_{jt}^k \mathrm{f}_k(c_{ijt}) . \tag{21}$$

Substituting for B_j^k and W_i^k we obtain

$$T_{ijt}^k = E_{jt}^k \left\{ \frac{\sum_i a_g^k \left(N_{igt} / \sum_g N_{igt} \right) r_{it} L_{it}^v Q_{it} \mathrm{f}_k(c_{ijt})}{\sum_i \left[\sum_g a_g^k \left(N_{igt} / \sum_g N_{igt} \right) \right] r_{it} L_{it}^v Q_{it} \mathrm{f}_k(c_{ijt})} \right\} . \tag{22}$$

Thus the required data are

T_{ijt}^k the number of persons of type k employed in area j and living in area i at time t,

E_{jt}^k the number of persons of type k employed in zone j at time t,

N_{igt} the number of households of type g living in zone i at time t,

r_{it} residential density (households acre^{-1}) in zone i at time t,

L_{it}^v vacant, developable land in zone i at time t,

Q_{it} a development index, as described above, for zone i, and

c_{ijt} travel cost (impedance) between the centroids of zones i and j at time t.

A further problem occurs with the definitions of T_{ijt}^k, E_{jt}^k, and N_{igt}. E_{jt}^k is defined as number of persons of type k working in zone j at time t, and T_{ijt}^k is the number of persons of type k employed in area j and living in area i at time t. However, N_{igt} is the number of households of type g living in zone i at time t. Clearly a conversion from employees to households is necessary at some point in the process. In order to simplify the conversion of T_{ijt}^k to vehicle trips for use in the network model, it will be most convenient to make the conversion at the residence end of the trip. Thus a matrix for converting households of type g to employees of type k must be developed from regional data for the regions to which the model is being fitted. This was done when the model was applied to San Francisco and Minneapolis–St Paul, but the use of these regional conversion rates across the board makes it necessary to keep careful track of this conversion throughout the calibration process.

Calibration results: partial estimates

Initially, it was intended that before the complete model equation was fitted, preliminary estimates of its parameters would be developed by partial estimation of them by least-squares regression. This was later found to be unnecessary, but some of the results related to the independent fitting of the trip distribution are of some interest.

It will be recalled that in equations (2) and (4) above, the distance functions used in the Lowry model and in PLUM were given. These are but two of a vast number of functions that could be fitted to trip-making data (March, 1971). To test several of these, a tabulation of the first work trips from the San Francisco Home Interview data file was prepared. These trips were tabulated according to the household and employment classes, enumerated earlier, for the 291 zone areal system. The distributions were then normalized and the resulting distributions were fitted, using a nonlinear least-squares procedure, to several different functions. The work-trip distributions took the familiar form shown in figure 1.

Of the various functions investigated, several types of the gamma distribution seemed to produce the best fits. The general form of this distribution is

$$v = c^\alpha \exp[f(c)] , \qquad (23)$$

where
v is the number of trips, or trip frequency,
c is the trip time or cost.

The specific functions that best fitted the data were sometimes best in one household income class and sometimes best in another; no one function was best for all four income classes. The function selected for further work on this prototype was

$$v = c^\alpha \exp(-\beta c) . \qquad (24)$$

This function, known as Tanner's function, had been used in this type of model elsewhere (Cripps and Foot, 1969). The best-fit parameters for the 291 zone system in San Francisco are shown in table 1. These parameters in Tanner's function do yield the skewed, peaked, curve shown below.

In the calibrations described below, the San Francisco data were aggregated to a thirty-zone system, thus increasing to greater than eight minutes the three-minute average travel time between adjacent zones of

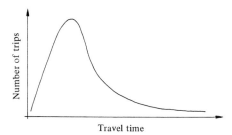

Figure 1. Typical intraurban work-trip distribution.

Table 1. Parameters of the work-trip function for San Francisco.

Income class ($)	α	β
0-4999	0·383	0·900
5000-9999	0·750	0·963
10000-14999	0·849	0·992
>15000	0·784	0·990

the 291 zone system. At that scale all the values of α become negative and Tanner's function takes on the appearance of a simple, declining exponential function. For the Minneapolis–St Paul calibration (approximately a 100 zone system) the level of disaggregation is sufficient for α to be positive again and for the skewed peaked curve to reappear. All of this reinforces the proposition that the level of spatial aggregation, or disaggregation, has noticeable effects on the apparent functional forms of these models.

Calibration results: complete estimates for San Francisco

The preliminary estimates of parts of the model were of very little use, except that they indicated that a product formulation for W would probably yield better fits than the sum form initially proposed; consequently equation (22) was rewritten. First, let

$$ W_{it}^k = \left[\prod_g \left(\frac{N_{it}^g}{\sum_g N_{it}^g} \right)^{a_g^k} \right] \left[\prod_m (X_{it}^m)^{a_m^k} \right] , \tag{25} $$

where

N_i^g is the number of type g households in area i, and
X_i^m is a measure of attribute m of zone i.

It was hoped that the attractiveness measure would continue to include intrinsic neighborhood attractiveness, as indicated by the household types located there, a measure of 'capacity' for development, and a measure of developability in terms of infrastructure. Various attributes were tested, including residential density, vacant developable land, percentage of developable land developed, and percentage of industrial (basic) land.

The variables that were finally selected are

n_i^k the percentage of the total households in zone i which are of type k,
L_i^v the available, developable land in zone i,
L_i^d the percentage of developable land in zone i which has been developed, and
r_i the residential density (households acre^{-1}) in zone i.

Thus the form of W used in the final calibrations was (using four household types)

$$ W_{it}^k = \left[\prod_{g=1}^{4} (n_i^g)^{a_g} \right] (L_i^v)^{a_5} (L_i^d)^{a_6} (r_i)^{a_7} . \tag{26} $$

Note that, based on the preliminary estimates, it was decided to replace the development-level factor, Q_i, by a simple measure of existing level of development, L_i^d.

Then, rewriting equation (22) we get

$$ T_{ijt}^k = E_{jt}^k \left[\frac{W_{it}^k \, f(c_{ijt})}{\sum_i W_{it}^k \, f(c_{ijt})} \right] . \tag{27} $$

Now there are two ways in which the parameters may be estimated. First, the simplest case, is by looking at the distribution(s) of the activities. In this case, $\sum_j T_{ijt}^k$ is the number of households of class k living in i, by definition. Thus

$$N_{it}^k = \sum_j E_{jt}^k \left[\frac{W_{it}^k f(c_{ijt})}{\sum_i W_{it}^k f(c_{ijt})} \right].$$

$$(28)$$

Consequently it is possible to estimate the parameters in the functions W and $f(c)$, and this may be called calibration of the aggregated form of the model.

However, various authors have asserted that there are disadvantages in calibrating the aggregated form of the model. Their remedy for these problems involves calibration of the disaggregated form of the model given in equation (27). It is an unfortunate fact that in order to calibrate the disaggregated form of the model it is necessary to have a good source of trip data. In the work described here there were questions about the quality of these data. If, at some later date, these questions can be satisfactorily resolved, along with the development of an acceptable expansion of the San Francisco 'sample' to an estimate of the 'population', then a calibration of the disaggregated form may be undertaken. In the meantime, calibration has been undertaken for the aggregated form of the model only.

It is immediately obvious that equation (28) cannot be fitted to a data set by using the traditional procedures of linear or even nonlinear multiple regression. In fact the only procedures available are those which, by some efficient procedure, search for the parameters that produce the best fit of the model to the data. One such procedure is that of gradient search, which involves the following steps:
(1) definition of a criterion function to be maximized or minimized;
(2) definition of the partial derivatives of the criterion function with respect to each of the parameters;
(3) selection of a starting point (parameters) and calculation of the criterion and the derivatives, hence the gradient, at that point;
(4) alteration of the parameters as a function of the calculated derivatives and gradient, and iteration until a minimum or maximum has been reached.

While this may sound like a rather lengthy and difficult undertaking, this is not actually the case. The computer software is somewhat difficult, but is available from a variety of sources, including the University of Pennsylvania. At this stage in its development it requires experienced staff for its proper use; nevertheless, once set up, the procedure is rather straightforward and results may be quickly obtained.

The San Francisco data were aggregated into a thirty-zone areal system primarily for economy of operation in the face of no previous experience of the costs and difficulties of performing such calibrations. It was felt that the thirty-zone system would take less computer time to calibrate although still providing useful information about both the model and the calibration process in general.

The model to be fitted is given in equation (28) and the distance function is that of equation (24). The variables in the attractiveness measure are those that were used in equation (25). The calibration was achieved with surprisingly little difficulty, and once the programs were operating correctly, there were no significant problems encountered. An interesting point is that a broad, flat ridge in n-space was found where the search program's criterion value, R^2, was somewhat insensitive to parameter variations. This was an expected occurrence, as suggested earlier (Batty, 1970); nonetheless, with patience, a maximum was reached. The parameters found are shown in table 2.

There are a number of observations to be made about these parameter values, the most important being that, before leaping to unwarranted conclusions, it must be remembered that the household data used in these runs are from the 1960 census, whereas the land-use and employment data are from surveys conducted in San Francisco in 1965. Thus the time subscripts for these variables are not correct for the formulation of the model. The purpose of this particular effort was to explore the problems of calibration of the derivatives of the Lowry model via the Wilson entropy approach; that this is a practical procedure has been amply demonstrated.

Table 2. Best-fit parameters (exponents)—DRAM—for San Francisco (thirty zones).

Household type ($)	Household composition				Land development			Distance		r^2
	a_1^k	a_2^k	a_3^k	a_4^k	a_5	a_6	a_7	α	β	
<5000	1·90	0·40	−0·50	0·33	0·18	−0·73	−0·26	−2·06	0·57	0·91
5000–10000	0·06	1·65	−1·22	0·48	0·27	−1·50	−0·07	−1·75	0·72	0·87
10000–15000	0·14	1·09	−0·26	0·76	0·24	−1·34	−0·14	−1·76	0·76	0·90
>15000	0·72	1·00	−0·34	1·50	0·23	−1·48	−0·04	−1·64	0·48	0·93

Calibration results: complete estimates for Minneapolis–St Paul

The DRAM model was also calibrated for an available data base for the Minneapolis–St Paul metropolitan area which was divided into one hundred and eight zones. The form of the equation used was also that of equation (28), with the distance function given by equation (24). The household income classes differed from those of San Francisco in that they were income quartiles. One of the attractiveness measures, r^i (residential density), was replaced by L_i^r (residential land), which produced better fits; the results of these estimates are shown in table 3.

The data used in this case are all from about 1970, thus resulting in parameter estimates for a static form of the model. It is interesting to note that the scaling or control-total procedures, typically used in these models after the allocations are completed, have moved, with the DRAM reformulation, deeper into the workings of the model. Referring to equation (27) it may be seen that the term in brackets on the right hand side is a proportion. Consequently each E_{jt}^k is simply allocated over all i zones, and, thus, the sum of N_i^k will be equal to the sum of E_j^k. It was mentioned above that it was necessary to convert E_j^k from employees of type k to heads of households of type k. If it is assumed that E_j^k sum to a prespecified regional employment total (or are forced to do so) then N_i^k can be forced to sum to a regional population total as part of the conversion from employees to heads of households. This, while still arbitrary, is not as arbitrary as the various forms of scaling procedure typically used in these models, which often involve altering sophisticated model estimates with rather crude pro rata procedures that vitiate the results of the model.

Table 3. Best-fit parameters (exponents)—DRAM—for Minneapolis–St Paul (one hundred and eight zones).

Household type	Household composition				Land development			Distance		r^2
	a_1^k	a_2^k	a_3^k	a_4^k	a_5	a_6	a_7	α	β	
First quartile	0·77	0·14	−0·56	−0·34	−0·03	0·15	0·89	1·04	2·18	0·93
Second quartile	0·24	0·84	−0·37	−0·15	−0·04	0·18	0·90	2·11	1·46	0·90
Third quartile	0·09	0·16	0·50	−0·08	−0·08	0·25	0·80	2·81	1·31	0·90
Fourth quartile	0·13	0·10	−0·19	0·78	−0·03	0·29	0·75	2·10	1·44	0·91

Discussion—problems of calibrations

The work described here was originally undertaken simply to explore the possibility of calibrating a Lowry-derivative model with a multivariate attractiveness measure via the Wilson entropy formulation. That this is possible has been amply demonstrated, but problems with the available data, particularly with respect to their time indices, make interpretation of the results somewhat chancy.

The general question of parameter interpretation in models of this form is worth discussing. First note that the scale of any of the variables is immaterial since the effect of the balancing factor, defined by equation (11), will be to normalize each variable in all cases. Thus parameters may be interpreted in terms of a variable which ranges from zero to one. Care must be taken to avoid having a variable reach zero if its exponent is negative, and checks should be incorporated in both parameter estimation and forecasting programs to alert the user, at the least, to this situation if it should arise.

In figure 2 several members of the family of curves of the form $v = c^\alpha$ are plotted for different values of α. The range in which we are particularly interested is from $c = 0$ to $c = 1$. Taking first the case of $\alpha \geq 0$, we see that for any α the value of v is less than unity. Thus any variable c_i, for which the estimated α is less than unity, will have an attenuating effect on the region's share of households in area i. This attenuation gradually diminishes as the value of c_i increases from zero to one. It is important to note that the intuitive expectation of a variable that has a positive exponent as an amplifying variable is not quite correct here. In the case of a variable whose range is zero to one, a positive exponent implies decreasing attenuation, with increases in the magnitude of the variable to its limit of unity. The case of $\alpha < 0$ produces considerable amplification for very small values of c, with the amount of amplification decreasing as c increases to its limit of one. Again, the intuitive motion

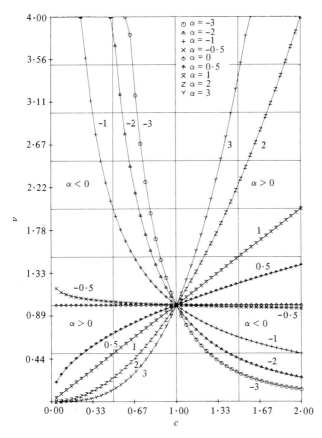

Figure 2. Plots of $v = c^\alpha$ for $0 < c < 2$ and $\alpha = -3, -2, -1, -0.5, 0, 0.5, 1, 2, 3$.

of a variable with a negative exponent being an attenuating variable is not quite correct. For the case of variables whose range is zero to one, a negative exponent implies decreasing amplification as the variable goes from zero to its limit of unity.

In the static situation, it makes more sense to consider each zone vis-à-vis all other zones. For a variable with a positive value of α, all other variables being equal, one would expect greater values of the dependent variable to be associated with greater values of the independent variable that has a positive α. Similarly, smaller values of the dependent variable would be expected to be associated with greater values of the independent variable that has a negative α. This reasoning also holds for the situation in which the particular independent variable increases or decreases. Nonetheless, it must be remembered that interpretation of the model's parameters does involve the notions that a decrease in attenuation produces increases and a decrease in amplification produces decreases, and that these are, to a certain degree, counter-intuitive.

In this same connection the use of the exponential-product form of the model caused some operating difficulties. These arise when one or another of the independent variables approaches zero. It may easily be seen in figure 1 that for values of c near zero the function $v = c^\alpha$ becomes rather volatile for all negative values of α. Consequently the Minneapolis–St Paul data were rerun with all the independent variables, with ranges from $0 \cdot 0$ to $1 \cdot 0$ shifted to the range $1 \cdot 0$ to $2 \cdot 0$ by simply replacing L_i^d, say, by $(1 \cdot 0 + L_i^d)$; these results are shown in table 4. Although there are some noticeable changes in the coefficients, as compared to the results in table 3, the overall patterns of coefficients are virtually identical. In this form both the problem of instability as the variables approach zero and the problem of the counter-intuitive operation of the exponents are remedied.

It is very difficult to refrain from speculating about the substantive implications of the parameters obtained in these estimations; nonetheless, this would be the wisest policy at this time. One cannot, however, resist the temptation to call attention to the household-composition variables and the interesting speculations that the reader may wish to make about them. Two questions are posed here which should be explored during

Table 4. Revised best-fit parameters (exponents)—DRAM—for Minneapolis–St Paul (one hundred and eight zones).

Household type	Household composition				Land development			Distance		r^2
	a_1^k	a_2^k	a_3^k	a_4^k	a_5	a_6	a_7	α	β	
First quartile	2·92	0·62	−1·71	−1·82	−0·10	0·55	0·83	0·92	2·14	0·89
Second quartile	1·51	2·04	−1·36	−1·57	−0·06	0·65	0·85	2·24	1·36	0·88
Third quartile	0·03	0·45	1·06	−0·64	−0·09	0·60	0·87	2·84	1·32	0·89
Fourth quartile	−0·54	−0·55	−0·06	1·13	−0·07	0·63	0·88	2·48	1·52	0·86

further work with the model. First, with regard to these parameters of the household composition in each zone, is there an apparent preference amongst household types for 'equals' or 'betters', that is, higher income classes? Further, if this preference appears, is it a preference for the amenities with which they are associated? Second, having seen how a change in the size of the areal unit changes the shape of the travel function, how does such a change affect that part of the model that deals with attractiveness? To the extent that the household compositions are representative measures of a complex of variables, their meaning may be lost on large areas. For example, the representation of neighborhood, which may show up at a small area level, may disappear when the areas are aggregated to larger zones.

Another set of questions that must be resolved during further work with this model is concerned with the interaction between the 'travel' parameters and the 'attractiveness' parameters. In these experiments one might first constrain the attractiveness parameters to zero and observe the fit of data to the travel function only, within the construct of the model. Then the reverse could be explored by constraining the travel parameters to zero and observing the fit of data to the attractiveness function only. This information might have been obtained from the independent fitting of the two parts of the model formulation described earlier. However, the functions used were not quite correct, nor were the data.

In retrospect it seems that the earlier, independent estimation of portions of the model that was performed for the San Francisco data was unnecessary in terms of estimating starting values of parameters for the complete model. The knowledge obtained about the appropriate functional forms to be used in the complete model was, however, a worthwhile result. In future calibration work with this model it will probably be more efficient to begin with the complete form of the model, perhaps omitting some of the attractiveness variables, or at least constraining their parameter values for the first few runs, while initial values of the other parameters are determined. This procedure seemed to work reasonably well for the Minneapolis–St Paul data. Finally, it should be noted that the use of r^2 as the criterion for parameter fitting is not clearly the best criterion for functional forms like DRAM. The use of maximum-likelihood criteria is being investigated for future work.

In conclusion, the initial tests of this model formulation are quite promising. The model appears to be capable of providing direct spatial allocations of households, by several types, without the need for complex input variables or involved sets of constraints and adjustments that are usually found at the tail-end of land-use models. Work is currently underway to reevaluate much of the work described here and to produce a more final and definitive form and calibration of DRAM.

Acknowledgements. This work was supported by the National Science Foundation, and, in part, by the US Department of Transportation, via Grant APR 73-07840-A02, "Development of an improved transportation and land use model package".

A large portion of the computer work that was necessary to produce these results was done by F Ducca, a graduate student in the Department. Earlier work on fitting portions of the models was done by C Sawyer and R Mathie, both graduate students in the Department.

References

Barras R, Broadbent T A, Cordey-Hayes M, Massey Doreen B, Robinson Krystyna, Willis J, 1971 "An operational urban development model of Cheshire" *Environment and Planning* 3 115-234

Batty M, 1970 "Some problems of calibrating the Lowry model" *Environment and Planning* 2 95-114

Batty M, 1972 "Recent developments in land-use modelling: a review of British research" *Urban Studies* 9 (2) 151-177

Batty M, Mackie S, 1972 "The calibration of gravity, entropy, and related models of spatial interaction" *Environment and Planning* 4 205-233

Crecine J, 1964 "A time-oriented metropolitan model for spatial location", Department of City Planning, Pittsburgh, Pennsylvania

Crecine J, 1969 "Spatial location decisions and urban structure: a time-oriented model", DP-4, Institute of Public Policy Studies, University of Michigan, Ann Arbor, Michigan

Cripps E L, Foot D H S, 1969 "The empirical development of an elementary residential location model for use in sub-regional planning" *Environment and Planning* 1 81-90

Goldner W, 1971 "The Lowry model heritage" *Journal of the American Institute of Planners* 37 100-110

Hyman G M, 1969 "The calibration of trip distribution models" *Environment and Planning* 1 105-112

Lowry I, 1964 "A model of metropolis" RM-4035-RC, Rand Corporation, Santa Monica, California

March L, 1971 "Urban systems: a generalized distribution function" in *London Papers in Regional Science 2. Urban and Regional Planning*, Ed. A G Wilson (Pion, London) pp 157-170

Putman S H, 1973 "The interrelationships of transportation development and land development", 2 volumes, Department of City and Regional Planning, University of Pennsylvania, Philadelphia, Pa

Putman S H, 1975 "Urban land use and transportation models: a state-of-the-art summary" *Transportation Research* 9 187-202

Senior M, 1973 "Approaches to residential location modelling 1: urban ecological and spatial interaction models (a review)" *Environment and Planning* 5 165-197

Voorhees A M, and Associates, 1972 "Application of the urban systems model (USM) to a region—North Central Texas", prepared for North Central Texas Council of Government

Wilson A G, 1967 "A statistical theory of spatial distribution models" *Transportation Research* 1 253-269

Wilson A G, 1970 "Disaggregating elementary residential location models" *Papers of the Regional Science Association* 14 103-125

On Hierarchical Dynamics

W.ISARD
University of Pennsylvania

In an earlier paper (Isard, 1976a), I speculated on theoretical developments that are necessary in regional science. One of the basic topics I identified was *hierarchical dynamics*, and in this paper I want to pursue this subject further. I want to discuss the theory that takes the tree from any particular hierarchical structure, such as that shown in figure 1, to another involving one more level of nodes—that is, the dynamics of the tree's development, or the tree's *morphogenesis*.

To make the problem of hierarchical dynamics clearer, let me pose it in several different ways. First, I would like to consider a paper by Vanwynsberghe (1976), presented at the Budapest meetings of the Regional Science Association in August 1975. Figure 2 draws upon some of his ideas for a three-tiered intersectoral model for Belgium. Involved were

Figure 1. An organization tree.

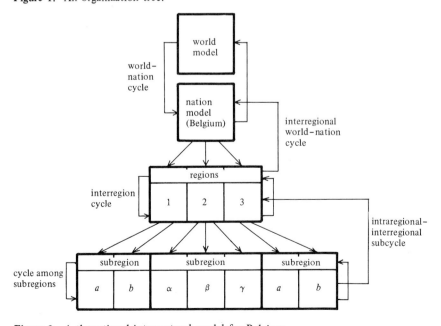

Figure 2. A three-tiered intersectoral model for Belgium.

nations whose economies were related via national exports and imports at
the world level, regions within each nation whose interconnections were
captured by an interregional input–output framework, and subregions
within each region linked by a migration and interareal commuting
framework. Realistically, such a model implies some form of world
authority or institution governing trade. Whether such an institution
comes to resemble the International Monetary Fund, the World Bank, or
something else much stronger, it is clear that it will surely condition
significantly the structure of import–export trade and world economy.
This same conclusion is reached when we examine carefully the policy
implications of the LINK econometric model which is currently undergoing
rapid development and whose interconnections can also be sketched by
figure 2[1]. This model will involve international authorities for policy
implementation, and these in turn will greatly influence the evolving world
economic structure.

Second, we can focus upon a *global balanced regional input–output*
model. This has already been proposed as an operational framework to
treat the awesome development programmes of nuclear energy confronting
the diverse regions of the world. At Budapest, I presented a brief report
on my research on nuclear-energy centers and made the point that the
location of nuclear-energy parks—each one perhaps of 50-100 GW capacity,
each containing the equivalent of 500 to 1000 power plants of the standard
100000 kW capacity—must be conceived as an *international* location
decision to be made or controlled by a global authority (Isard, 1976b). A
global balanced regional input–output model designed to give decision-

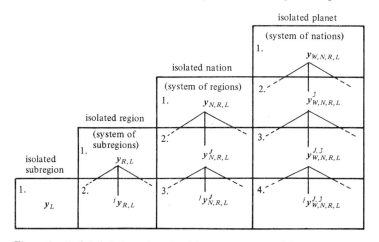

Figure 3. A global, balanced regional input–output model.

[1] In figure 2, we might let the nation be the USA, the regions, North, South, and
West, and the subregions, New York State, Pennsylvania, etc.

makers crude, but early, answers to the question of impact is sketched in figure 3, with appropriate symbols for output vectors in each box.

[The equations for solving for the outputs of local, regional, and national commodities in each local area, region, and the nation as a whole for the isolated nation system (and also for an isolated region or subregion system) have been presented on a number of occasions. For example, see Leontief et al. (1953, chapters 4 and 5) and Isard et al. (1969, pages 869–871). Using the notation in Isard et al. and letting W represent world commodities (commodities whose supply and demand balance on the world level only), J represent nations, and ${}^{j}\mathbf{\mathcal{C}}^{J,\,J}$ represent an appropriate diagonal matrix of constants, we can solve for the output vector ${}^{j}y^{J,\,J}$ for each subregion $j, j = 1, ..., \bar{j}$, in each region $J, J = A, ..., U$, of each nation $J, J = A, ..., V$, in the isolated planet system as follows,

$$
{}^{j}y_{W}^{J,\,J} = {}^{j}\mathbf{\mathcal{C}}^{J,\,J} \left|\mathbf{A}_{W}d\right.
$$

$$
{}^{j}y_{N}^{J,\,J} = {}^{j}\mathbf{C}^{J,\,J}{}_{N}\left|\mathbf{A}_{\widetilde{W}\widetilde{W}}(d_{\widetilde{W}}^{J} + \mathbf{A}_{\widetilde{W}W}\, y_{W}^{J})\right.
$$

$$
{}^{j}y_{R}^{J,\,J} = {}^{j}\mathbf{K}^{J,\,J}{}_{R}\left|\mathbf{A}_{\widetilde{N}\widetilde{N}}(d_{\widetilde{N}}^{J,\,J} + \mathbf{A}_{\widetilde{N}N}\, y_{N}^{J,\,J} + \mathbf{A}_{\widetilde{N}W}\, y_{W}^{J,\,J})\right.
$$

$$
{}^{j}y_{L}^{J,\,J} = \left|\mathbf{A}_{LL}({}^{j}d_{L}^{J} + \mathbf{A}_{LR}\,{}^{j}y_{R}^{J} + \mathbf{A}_{LN}\,{}^{j}y_{N}^{J} + \mathbf{A}_{LW}\,{}^{j}y_{W}^{J})\right.
$$

where
$\mathbf{A}$ represents the matrix of technical coefficients
$|\mathbf{A} = (\mathbf{I}-\mathbf{A})^{-1}$, the Leontief inverse matrix
d represents a vector of final demand
${}^{j}\mathbf{C}^{J,\,J}, {}^{j}\mathbf{\mathcal{C}}^{J,\,J}, {}^{j}\mathbf{K}^{J,\,J}$ represent diagonal matrices of constants.
W represents world commodities $\widetilde{N}$ represents nonnational commodities
$\widetilde{W}$ represents nonworld commodities R represents regional commodities
N represents national commodities L represents local commodities.]

Clearly, nuclear power must be conceived of as an *international* (world) commodity in this framework. However, which other goods turn out to be international and which remain national, regional, and local again depends, in a significant manner, on the type of world institution and authority that emerges.

Third, we can consider the hierarchical dynamics problem with respect to the history of general equilibrium frameworks in regional science. At the extreme left of the lower part of figure 4 [2] is, first, a framework of an exchange economy, after Walras, consisting of m consumers and a single region. Second, there is a framework of a production economy with n producers, m consumers, and a single region. Third, there is a framework of a multiregion trade economy with $\bar{f}$ shippers, n producers, and m consumers in each of U regions (see Isard et al, 1969, chapter 11). Fourth, there is a framework of a multiregion welfare economy with $\bar{d}$ governments, $\bar{f}$ shippers, n producers, and m consumers in each of U regions (see Isard et al, 1969, chapters 13 and 14). Finally, from this year's research, there is a framework of a U-region world system with a central planning agency as part of a world governmental unit, and with $\bar{d}$ governments, $\bar{f}$ shippers, n producers, and m consumers in each region (see Isard and Liossatos, 1975). I have presented the comparative statics

[2] For the moment, ignore the upper part of figure 4. The lower part of this figure and the accompanying discussion is taken from my Budapest paper (Isard, 1976b).

analysis for each of these five systems; but nowhere have I been able to analyze the process of transition from any one of these systems to the next, or how the transition itself influences the structure of the resulting system.

Recently, Prigogine et al. (1972) have put forward some thought provoking ideas. They have noted the apparent contradiction between biological order and the laws of physics (in particular the second law of thermodynamics), and that this contradiction cannot be resolved so long as we try to understand living systems (*and I add social systems*) by the methods of the familiar equilibrium statistical mechanics, and equally familiar thermodynamics. One of the main conclusions of their theory is that there exists a class of systems exhibiting two kinds of behavior:

(1) a tendency to the state of maximum disorder (entropy) for one type of situation; and

(2) coherent behavior, which involves increasing hierarchical and spatial order over time.

According to Prigogine et al. (1972, page 24), "the destruction of order always prevails in the neighborhood of thermodynamic equilibrium. In contrast, *creation* of order may occur far from equilibrium ... beyond the domain of stability of the states that have the usual thermodynamic properties ... . The best known examples of this duality in behavior are instabiliities in fluid dynamics, such as the onset of thermal convection in a fluid layer heated from below. For a critical value of the external constraint (temperature gradient), that is, beyond a critical distance from equilibrium, an instability arises that causes the spontaneous emergence of

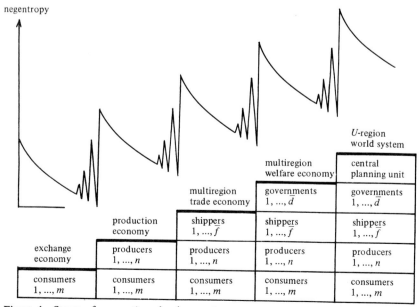

Figure 4. Stages of space–time development.

convection patterns. Below the instability threshold, the energy of the system is distributed in the random thermal motion of the molecules". Here, any fluctuation would give rise to small convection currents that would be damped. But beyond instability the energy of the system appears partly as the energy of macroscopic convection patterns; and the system acts to amplify fluctuations, to drive the average values of the system to a new regime. Prigogine et al. (1972, pages 23–25) speak of the principle of *order through fluctuation.*

If I were now to suggest a crude, but simple, way of integrating some of Prigogine's ideas with the conceptual framework which has been developed in regional science, I would draw the series of curves in the upper half of figure 4. Time is measured along the horizontal axis of each of these curves, and negentropy, the negative of entropy, is measured along the vertical axis. For each of the five systems depicted we see that, with the passage of time, entropy increases and tends to a maximum —consistent with the second law of thermodynamics for an isolated system. However, the transition from one system to another in the series involves *coherent behavior* and a significant flow of energy from the outside world, leading to the creation of order of a degree greater than had ever existed previously and to a correspondingly higher state of negentropy. The notion of sharp, severe fluctuations in the transition period is suggested by the zig-zag lines between any two consecutive curves. According to Prigogine a model of this transition period should involve stochastic analysis.

Although we must refrain from employing directly models that biologists and other natural scientists have found useful, nonetheless, we can often gain considerable insight by attempting to construct parallel models. Certainly Prigogine's analysis exposes one fruitful line of thought with regard to combining concepts of entropy with general equilibrium models. These developments are being pursued further.

Let me give a brief preview of one specific probe. At Budapest I presented a simple optimal space–time development model (Isard and Liossatos, 1975), which is obtained by excluding the symbol, the terms, and equations in brackets in the system of equations below. Then I constructed, with Liossatos, an 'error-copy' variant of this model which is as follows (and which does include the symbol, the terms, and the equations in square brackets):

$$\dot{K} = F(K, u) - C - rK + [\epsilon F_1(K, K_A)] \,, \tag{1}$$

$$\dot{R} = \psi(C) - \rho R + [\epsilon \psi_1(C, K_A)] \,, \tag{2}$$

$$[\dot{K}_A = \epsilon G(K, v'(R), K_A)] \,, \tag{3}$$

with

$$C = C(K, R, [K_A]) \,,$$

where

$K\ [= K(t)]$ is the capital stock at time t,

$F(K, u)$ is the output of a single good from production at time t per unit of time,

$C\ [= C(t)]$ is the consumption at time t per unit of time,

r is the rate of depreciation of capital,

$R\ [= R(t)]$ is the level of pollution at time t,

$\psi(C)$ is the output of pollution (associated with consumption) at time t per unit of time,

ρ is the rate of decay of level of pollution,

$K_A\ [= K_A(t)]$ is the stock (accumulated production) of pollution control equipment at time t (which plays the role of 'error copy' of K),

$\epsilon F_1(K, K_A)$ is an adjustment to reflect the impact of the stock of K_A upon output of the single good,

$\epsilon \psi_1(C, K_A)$ is an adjustment to reflect the impact of the stock of K_A upon the output of pollution,

$\epsilon G[K, v'(R), K_A]$ is the production of K_A per unit of time, from K in association with R and K_A, $v'(R)$ playing the role of an enzyme,

$C(K, R)$ and $C(K, R, K_A)$ indicate how consumption is determined in terms of the state variables so as to maximize an objective, in our case social welfare.

Note that in this model the ordinary equations of motion, equations(1) and (2), which govern respectively the time rate of increase of capital and the stock of pollution, are each modified to include an error (perturbation) term. Also a third equation of motion, equation (3), governing the time rate of increase in the stock of pollution control equipment (capital), is introduced. In this model the basic parameter, u, the level of technology, plays a critical role. For relatively low values of u, the impact of any perturbation on the system is very small, and the magnitudes $K(t)$ and $R(t)$ stay close to the steady state $\{K^*, R^*\}$ which would characterize the asymptotically stable model obtained when the symbol, the terms, and the equation in brackets are eliminated from the above equation system. However, when the level of technology reaches a critical value $\bar{u}$, any random perturbation (fluctuation) around the structurally unstable steady state $\{\hat{K}^*, \hat{R}^*, 0\}$ of the above equation system becomes greatly magnified, such that the probability of moving into violent fluctuations and collapsing —or possibly reaching through guidance (or chance) a new steady state which is 'far away'—is high. Specifically, in the context of environmental management, when u takes the value $\bar{u}$ for which $\hat{R}^* = \bar{R}$, additional environmental degradation involves a sudden major disruption of the physical environment, a sudden adverse effect on the health of the population, or any other factor that leads to a sudden sharp increase in the marginal disutility, $v'(R)$, of pollution. Before this level was reached, there might have been a small, gradually increasing demand (perhaps with reference to only a few individuals) for abatement and thus for the installation of pollution control equipment. At $\overline{R}$, and slightly beyond it, there is a sudden sharp increase. As a result of this process, we expect, through proper guidance (or chance), the emergence of a new regime—a regime with a strong world government unit having, among other powers, the power to tax, to regulate world environment, and to force compliance by nations.

I believe I can illustrate even more forcefully the effectiveness of Prigogine's approach by referring to my early studies as an historian of the economic development of the United States (Isard, 1942a; 1942b; 1943; Isard and Isard, 1943). During the 19th century and the first half of the 20th century no technology had as great an impact as transport technology. Suppose we begin with the early decades of the 19th century. The first canals constructed were specific projects, designed to open up a coalfield, for example, and were, more or less, random perturbations. The completion of the Erie Canal in 1825, however, demonstrated conclusively that the canal could be a primary generalized mode of transport. The psychological effect was 'electric'. Without question the American economy was both greatly disrupted and propelled forward by this development, and subsequent canal networks were laid down. Major fluctuations in business activity, major revaluations of resources, major alterations of transportation flows, and shifts of population and industry took place. Eventually a new higher order of economy emerged, with New York City rather than Philadelphia as the primary node and with the region west of the Alleghenies no longer independently oriented to New Orleans but rather integrated within a new multiregion trade structure as part of the greater hinterland of the Eastern Seaboard.

The railroad came later. At first it represented a minor perturbation in the system. In a decade or so, the railroad was demonstrated to be profitable as an intraregional mode and still later as an interregional and transcontinental mode. The major fluctuations, resource revaluations, reorientation of trade and interconnections, and the tremendous growth of the United States economy which ensued, clearly testify to the emergence of a basically new regime. This new regime, with drastically altered structural relations, integrated the diverse regions of the United States around Chicago as the railroad hub.

Finally, the 20th century witnessed the automotive engine, first as a random perturbation, and then as a very widely adopted new technology. The tremendous repercussions which it has had on the urban structure of the major industrialized nations and their populations, and on the industrial and commercial distributions and patterns are all too familiar to bear repetition. That it has also been associated with a new 'regime' of social, economic, political, and cultural life is also self-evident.

To sum up, in each case of major transport innovation in the United States during the 19th century and the first half of the 20th century, a new order was created corresponding to a transition to a higher level of negentropy. This is consistent, in a very crude and broad manner, with the diagram in the upper half of figure 4 that is used to summarize some of Prigogine's ideas on "far from equilibrium" situations and the "principle of order through fluctuation". The canal, then the railroad, then the automotive engine: each might be viewed as having served as a specific catalyst, or enzyme, which facilitated the development of a new phase of socioeconomic and political life.

The above statements, although forceful and full of insight, are still only suggestive. They are much too broadly framed for the kind of scientific hypothesis testing that must be performed. The task of tightening up the theoretical basis of the kinds of systems that have been used to model the diverse aspects of the phenomena involved is now underway. This involves, at least, (1) the question of exit from a given regime, (2) the identification of the several or many possible structures of a new regime, (3) the attributes of a transition path. The problem of exit basically relates to the question of structural stability and instability, which must be distinguished from asymptotic stability (Isard and Liossatos, 1977; Rosen, 1970). The question of the structure of a possible new regime involves careful analysis of the characteristics of viable hierarchical structures and the identification of sets of desirable and consistent properties for such structures (Isard and Kaniss, 1976). The transition path involves the study of possible interim structural elements that may come to exist or in some cases must necessarily exist (Thom, 1974). Further basic research in all these directions is obviously required.

Acknowledgement. This research was supported by National Science Foundation grant P.251018.

References

Isard W, 1942a "Transport development and building cycles" *The Quarterly Journal of Economics* November 90-112

Isard W, 1942b "A neglected cycle: The transport-building cycle" *The Review of Economic Statistics* **XXIV** November 149-158

Isard W, 1943 *The Economic Dynamics of Transport Technology* unpublished Ph D dissertation, Harvard University Archives, Cambridge, Mass.

Isard W, 1975 "Notes on an evolutionary theoretic approach to world organization" *Papers, Peace Science Society (International)* 24 113-124

Isard W, 1976a "Some directions for the extension of dynamic spatial analysis" in *London Papers in Regional Science 6. Theory and practice in Regional Science* Ed. I Masser (Pion, London) pp 1-10

Isard W, 1976b "On regional science models: Parallels from biological science" *Papers, Regional Science Association* 37 (Budapest meetings)

Isard W, Isard C, 1943 "The transport-building cycle in urban development: Chicago" *The Review of Economic Statistics* **XXV** November 224-226

Isard W, Kanemoto Y, 1976 "On an elementary model of the development of urban systems" *Papers, Regional Science Association* 36

Isard W, Kaniss P, 1976 "Summary of selected writings on hierarchical theories" *Papers, Peace Science Society (International)* 27 and unpublished manuscript

Isard W, Liossatos P, 1975 "General micro behavior and optimal macro space-time planning" *Regional Science and Urban Economics* **5** 287-323

Isard W, Liossatos P, 1977 "Models of transition processes" *Papers of the Regional Science Association* **38**

Isard W, Smith T, and others 1969 *General Theory: Social, Political, Economic and Regional* (MIT Press, Cambridge, Mass.)

Leontief W, and others 1953 *Studies in the Structure of the American Economy* (Oxford University Press, New York)

Prigogine I, Nicolis G, Babloyantz A, 1972 "Thermodynamics of evolution" *Physics Today* november 23-28; December 28-44

Rosen R, 1970 *Dynamical System Theory in Biology* (John Wiley, New York)

Thom R, 1974 *Structural Stability and Morphogenesis* (Benjamin, Reading, Mass.)

Vanwynsberghe D, 1976 "Missile: An international driven multi-interregional intersectoral model for Belgium" (mimeo)

Urban Simulation—The Vancouver Experience

M.GOLDBERG
University of British Columbia

1 Introduction: objectives and overview of the work
1.1 History

Nearly seven years ago a number of colleagues and I set out to develop a large-scale simulation model with the participation of several levels of government and broad interdisciplinary cooperation within our university. This paper describes that project and some of its strengths and weaknesses.

The project was first conceived in the winter of 1969–1970 at the close of a decade of fairly intense but relatively inconclusive urban-simulation efforts. The initial conception derived from a concern for environmental issues relating to urban regions as opposed to the more traditional concern for transportation/land-use issues. The original proposal reflects these concerns:

"Significant advances have recently been made in bridging disciplines concerned with the interactions between man and environment. The success of these efforts now suggests the need for a bridge between those institutions which formulate and those which implement policies. If policy decisions are to be influenced, institutional boundaries must be crossed. The logical extension of the interdisciplinary approach is, therefore, an inter-institutional one. By bridging both institutions and disciplines, it is hoped that not only will questions be posed in a multidimensional way, but, more importantly, that solutions will be evaluated against a similar diversity of criteria. The inter-institutional approach provides the flexibility to expand the frames of reference for defining, solving, and above all implementing solutions to 'the problem'.... We believe, therefore, that this will make our study much more than just a link in the evolution of urban models and forecasting efforts" (Goldberg and Holling, 1970, pages 1 and 3).

Accordingly our emphasis was on applied work which would shed light on a number of systemic problems and solutions facing the Vancouver region. This general concern to provide assistance in making urban environmental decisions led us to develop two broad sets of subgoals.

The first of these related to usability. We felt that our work must be simultaneously useful, usable, and above all used. By useful we meant that the inputs and outputs had to be informational items that were similar to those actually used by decisionmakers. Policy variables and policy interventions in particular had to parallel closely those policies likely to be implemented in the real world which the models attempt to mimic.

Our second criterion was that the models be usable. By this we meant that they had to be economical to run, reasonably easy to understand and use for policy experiments, and easily accessible to as wide an audience as possible, including the lay public. (This is similar to the notion of transparency that Lee, 1973, develops.)

Finally, and most importantly, we felt that it was essential that the models actually be used. Only with use and application to current questions could the models be refined and revised. This process of use, revision, etc, is summarized in figure 1, which is an idealization of the model-building process.

Our second principal subgoal related to holism. We felt quite strongly that where a trade-off was necessary we should opt for holism and synthesis instead of rigorous analysis. The world we live in is in all likelihood never completely knowable. Accordingly, our decisions cannot include all relevant data, nor can our models. Our models are abstractions from reality and as such must selectively exclude some of the complexity and richness of the environments we are attempting to simulate. This respect for our ignorance and a desire to provide meaningful inputs for the decisionmaking process led us to choose the broad brush over the microscope (for example, holism over rigour) where such a choice was needed. By taking such a stand we felt that we were also providing a better framework for undertaking good rigorous analysis, since we were creating a synthetic structure into which these analyses might be imbedded

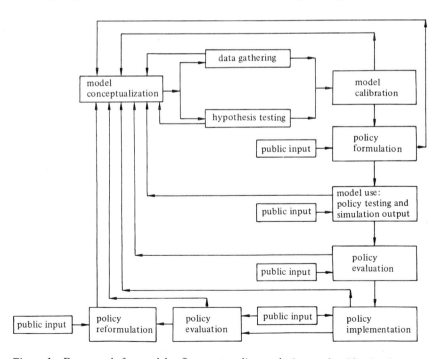

Figure 1. Framework for model refinement, policy evolution, and public involvement.

both for a better understanding of relatively narrowly specified phenomena and for the treatment of broader systemic questions.

To achieve these goals we decided that it was necessary to include decisionmakers in the model-development process from the outset. We envisioned extending the interdisciplinary approaches of the 1960s into the realm of interinstitutional cooperation and participation. (Hence the name, 'Inter-Institutional Policy Simulator' or IIPS.)

1.2 Interinstitutional cooperation

The ideas underlying this interinstitutional approach are summarized in figure 2, which illustrates the evolution of interdisciplinary research to interinstitutional efforts on through to public involvement in the decision-making processes of society.

Interinstitutional participation was viewed as a means of achieving our goals. First, working closely with decisionmakers would force our work to be synthetic. It would have to include and transcend the short-run pragmatism of decisionmakers and the longer-run idealism and rigour of academics. In addition, interinstitutional research would have to be useful, usable, and used if decisionmakers were going to be kept interested in the work, since they have little time for the elegant niceties of traditional academic projects.

By including people from a variety of government departments and from a number of different levels of government, the work would also be interdisciplinary since governments are arranged by and large along problem and policy foci, each of which usually spans a number of academic disciplines.

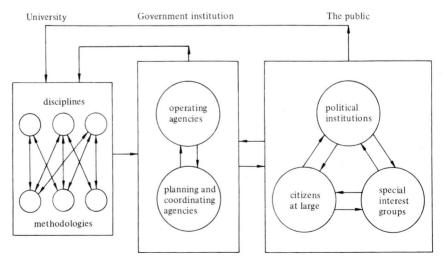

Figure 2. The model-building process: framework for interinstitutional and public involvement.

Finally, the interinstitutional framework provided a stimulus to a process-versus-product orientation for our work. We were very much afraid that our efforts would result in yet another magical forecasting and policymaking tool (a bigger and even blacker black box). The experiences of some of the early work in San Francisco made us very wary of creating an expensive tool in search of an appropriate problem to solve. By focusing on process (figure 1) we hoped to avoid the dangers inherent in developing a more powerful planning technology that would be used to justify decisions rather than to illuminate them. From our university base, a number of government departments were contacted to feel out their support for an interinstitutional project. The response was cautious at first but positive and evoked renewed efforts on our part. As a result of these efforts we were able to develop a formal working agreement between the university and three governments: the City of Vancouver (including the engineering, finance, planning, and social planning departments); the Greater Vancouver Region District (GVRD), a prototype regional government in the metropolitan area; and the Province of British Columbia (more specifically the BC Department of Municipal Affairs).

A five-year time horizon was chosen, as we felt that this represented a reasonable amount of time to develop, debug, and begin to use a set of models. It would also give the time needed to adapt the models to changing demands placed by decisionmakers.

The best laid plans, as we know, do not always succeed. The critical turning point was probably the entry of the federal government into the picture. In the summer of 1971 the Canadian federal government created a new agency to deal with urban policy and research. The agency was called the Ministry of State for Urban Affairs (MSUA). MSUA had a sizable research budget and was attracted to IIPS as a pilot project that might be transferable to other Canadian cities. Unlike the other levels of government, MSUA did not participate as a partner, but rather through a research contract. The contract was to run for an undetermined number of years and was to be renewed annually. The cost to the federal government was on the order of $200000 per year, compared with $372000 over five years from the Ford Foundation. The size of the budget and the contractual nature of the agreement violated both our philosophy of gradual evolution of the project and our emphasis upon process. Research contracts do not look for successful processes but rather require a successful product. The shift to a product orientation, and the federal government's disproportionate power (deriving from its disproportionate share of the budget) led to a change in the philosophy and development of the model system.

As a result of a continuous stream of federal site visitors and officials, a number of people who were centrally involved in the model-building exercise (including me) left the project in 1973. By December 1974 the federal government had severed its relationship with the project, thus

killing it.   At its timely death the project had on its payroll a project
director, a research director, half a dozen full-time programmers, a
secretarial staff, and a community-participation organizer (public relations)
with an annual price tag of nearly $200000 in total.   The project had
degenerated into an exercise in form with virtually no substance.   Process
had succumbed to rhetoric, and models were replaced by elaborate data
banks, graphic displays, and interactive software.   Many will disagree, but I
still believe IIPS was an idea whose time had come, and gone.   In our
original submission we had hoped to create an institution that knew when
to die.   If nothing else we achieved this goal.
     So much for history.   On with the show.

2 The models and their development
The foregoing sets out the framework within which the simulation work
described below was conducted.   Figure 3 depicts the simulation system
as it was initially conceived.   A detailed description of the model set can
be found in Goldberg (1973) and the various reports issued by the project
before its demise.
     The general philosophy for developing the models was initially one of
continuous evolution and refinement.   Flexibility and maximum room for

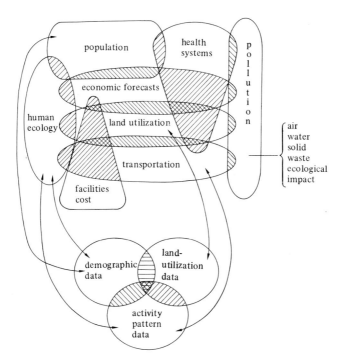

Figure 3. Diagram of relationships between the IIPS subgroups.

innovation and creativity were the fundamental rules to be followed. Thus, the model started with four components—population growth and migration, economic growth, transportation, and land use. Each of these models in turn was to be refined and, where relevant, whole parts replaced (as in the housing component of the land-use model). While this refinement and replacement of pieces was to be occurring in the initial model, other models were being developed in parallel. For example the health-care model operated on a stand-alone basis. It was to be linked later to the initial four submodels (see Milsum et al., 1971; Swoveland et al., 1973).

The other models—namely, water and air pollution, human ecology, and facilities costs—were in the conceptualization stage, and during the next several years were to move through stages of data collection, programming, and debugging, eventually interfacing (human ecology excluded) with the four components below.

3 The housing and land-use elements
Many of the subgroups described above either never got under way or else eventually split off on their own. What remained was a core of models centered on the land-use model set. It is this set (the principal module) that will be the centre of attention for the discussion here. Figure 4 sketches out the module as well as its interaction with the regional-transportation model.

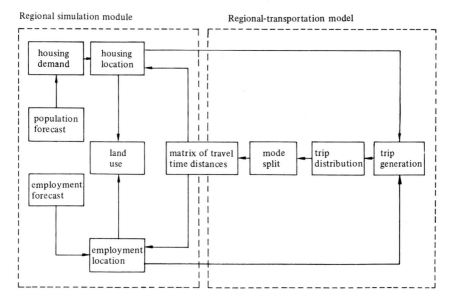

Regional simulation module   Regional-transportation model

Figure 4. The interaction between the module and the regional transportation model.

3.1 Land-use model overview
The principal focus of this section is the housing component of the land-use model. As the housing component is the best-developed component to date, it illustrates best the development strategy outlined earlier.

The land-use models are sketched out in figure 5 in their simplest detail. The right-hand side of the figure represents various supply elements, whereas the left-hand side depicts the two principal demand elements— land for jobs and houses. The conceptual structure is simple in these models in that activities (jobs and houses) are allocated to each of the eighty-two subareas in the Vancouver region via a number of algorithms (one algorithm associated with each activity). These allocations are then converted to land use via a land-absorbtion coefficient which represents the amount of land that a unit of each activity requires. If there is sufficient land for the activity, then it is considered to be allocated to that zone, and the land-use, employment, housing, and population files are all updated for that zone. If there is insufficient supply, the excesses are cumulated across all subareas and relocated, using the initial algorithms, to subareas with excess capacity. When all jobs and households are allocated to subareas for year t, a new set of forecasts from the population and economics models are read in for year $t+1$ and allocated as above until the module reaches the terminal year for its forecasting horizon.

The employment-location models follow closely earlier work in the field of urban model building (Goldberg, 1968; Putman, 1972) and as a result will not be described here in any detail.

3.2 Housing model: overview, detail, and evolution
In figure 6 we see the housing elements set out in a fashion similar to that used in figure 5 for the land-use elements. The housing-demand elements are grouped roughly on the left-hand side of the diagram, and the housing-supply elements appear on the right. The market-resolution process is set out in the centre of the figure. A brief overview of the demand, supply, and market processes is useful in order to understand the recent evolution of the models.

3.2.1 Step (1)
Demand. Initially for computational convenience it was assumed that supply equalled demand for the region as a whole. However, it was not assumed that supply and demand had to be equal in any of the eighty-two subareas, nor did we constrain regional totals for demand by structure type (single family, multiple family) or by value class (there are four value classes) to be equal to the equivalent regional totals for supply. All we assumed was that the total number of units demanded equalled the total number of units supplied in each period. Regional demand by structure type and value class is a function of family size and age distribution of household heads (from the population model) and of the income distribution (from the economic model), for each annual forecast

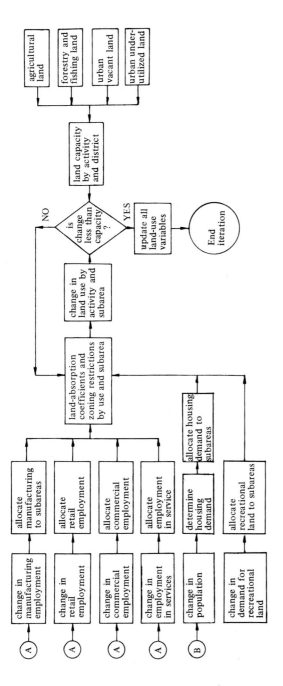

A   Employment changes from economic model

B   Change in population from population model

Figure 5. Land-use models.

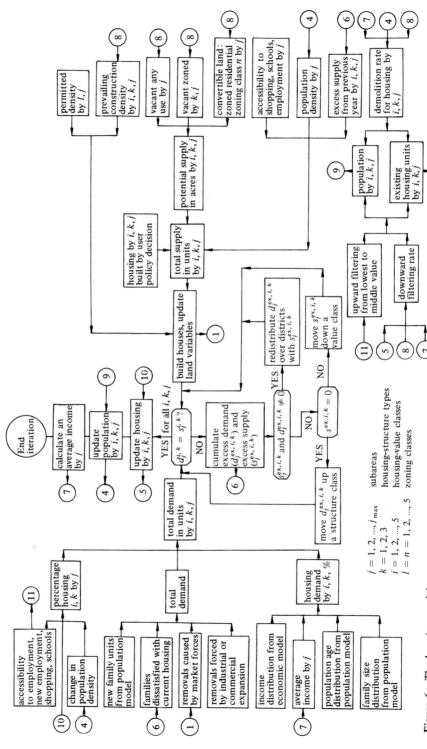

Figure 6. The housing model.

increment. In addition, demand derives from households whose housing units have been demolished during the previous period. Finally the initial model kept track of households that were forced into units other than they desired, and these dissatisfied households also entered into the calculation of demand. Given these regional totals for demand by value class and structure type, the microspatial model then allocated demand to each of the eighty-two subareas, again by value class and structure type. The resulting demand $d_j^{i, k}$ is demand in subarea j, for housing type k, value class i.

Prices are explicitly excluded from the demand (and supply) equations. This decision resulted from the immense complexity of forecasting subsequent period prices, which are a necessity if prices were to be given a central role in the model. Prices also carried with them the danger of implying a level of accuracy to which no simulation model can pretend. Elimination of prices made the models computationally more efficient and more usable, since users would not be lulled into a sense of precision that price forecasts often create.

Supply. Since supply was constrained to equal demand in this initial phase, the supply model took the number of units demanded for the region as its starting point. Thus the supply model proceeded from the total regional new supply of units and disaggregated this new supply into structure types, value classes, and subareas. The principal data inputs to this disaggregation procedure are actual and allowable densities, available land, accessibility, and excess supply by value class, structure type, and subarea from the previous iteration of the model. The result is supply $s_j^{i, k}$ by subarea area j, structure type k, and value class i.

Market resolution. Differences between supply and demand by structure type and value class for each subarea are reconciled by cumulating excess demand and redistributing it to areas with excess supply until there is no excess demand or excess supply in any subarea, structure type, or value class of housing. Excess demand $d_j^{\text{ex}, i, k}$, is allocated first to other subareas with similar housing (by type and class). If no similar housing is available, demand is allocated to those areas that have housing of the same value class but any structure type. If there is no such housing available, the excess is allocated to subareas with the originally desired structure type but the next lower value class. Such housing is thus raised a value class and reclassified in memory accordingly. This process continues until all excess demands are allocated. In this way an 'upward filtering' of both houses and neighbourhoods is achieved. If on the other hand there are excess supplies $s_j^{\text{ex}, i, k}$ in certain subareas, the excess housing is assigned to the next lower value class. In this way excess supply moves down through value classes, which is what happens in practice where high vacancy rates lead to price cutting. Excess demand, however, moves across structure types within the same value class unless no housing exists in any subarea in the desired value class, in which case demand moves down one value class and then across the structure types again if needed. Such a phenomenon has already been observed in Vancouver as well as in such newly stylish areas as Society Hill in Philadelphia, Cobble and Boerum Hills in Brooklyn, Russian Hill and Jackson Heights in San Francisco, and Capital Hill in Seattle. Upward filtering seems to be alive and well in many cities.

Excess demand and excess supply are both kept in memory for one period: the former to be used as a measure of dissatisfaction, the latter to introduce a dynamic lag into the supply-determination process.

3.2.2 Step (2)

The next step in the evolution of the model was to drop the assumption that demand and supply had to be equal for the region as a whole. Accordingly we adopted a very simple multiplier–accelerator-type model from macroeconomics. Demand was merely set equal to the forecast population divided by the number of persons per household (h) to yield an estimate of the number of households forecast for each time period. New supply s^n, on the other hand, was assumed equal to this change in the number of households N^h plus a demand for vacancies d^v to allow for equilibration of short-term disturbances (that is, some inventories for short-run adjustments) minus the housing supply. Equation (1) sets out the supply relationship:

$$s_t^n = N_t^h - S_t + v_t N_t^h \ . \tag{1}$$

The demand for vacancies in turn was assumed to be a function of vacancy rates in the proceeding three years (there being a three-year planning horizon for developers in our region). If s_t^n is negative then a small number of units is still built, reflecting the fact that construction does not cease even with high excess housing stocks.

3.2.3 Step (3)

This is the stage at which we are currently running the model. This step builds upon step (2) and continues to assume that regional demand for units and regional supply are not necessarily equal. Supply is again calculated as in step (2). Demand, however, is now calculated using feedback from the housing-location (microspatial) submodel. This is accomplished by using an index of saturation in each subarea, which is weighted by the amount of development already existing in that subarea.

The foregoing describes the structure of the models and in particular illustrates the evolution of the housing model and the development of a simple feedback mechanism linking macrospatial demand (that is, the regional total) with microspatial elements of land availability in each subarea. Accordingly we now proceed to a brief examination of the behaviour of the model under each of the steps in its evolution.

3.3 Output characteristics of the early model
There are two basic types of intervention that we can make with this model. The first is a *quantitative intervention* in which the magnitude of variables can be changed (for example land may be frozen), densities changed through a zoning policy, and changes made in transportation facilities thus affecting accessibilities. At our current spatial scale (82 subareas for a region of roughly 600 square miles) the infrastructure (utility placement) is not meaningful, since all 82 areas are serviced even though subareas within these might not be. The second is a *structural intervention* in which an alternative model form is chosen, for instance the saturation index can be used to change migration or housing demand. Any combination of these feedbacks may be switched on or off for a given model run. Figure 7 shows three different simulations under which structural interventions were made. In this figure, backlink represents the feedback from land-use to housing demand via the saturation index. The migration option applies the same index to migration flows. Differences demonstrate the effects of these various structural options.

We specifically avoided building in dynamically adjusting density and redevelopment algorithms. We felt that these kinds of options were the purview of decisionmakers and preferred to keep the models confined to 'if–then' type questions where 'if a rezoning (higher permissible density) then...' questions might be posed. The terminal year of the simulation thus becomes of interest to decisionmakers in their attempts to provide more housing and jobs.

Figure 8 shows the response of regional housing supply to various scenarios (qualitative interventions). The university endowment lands

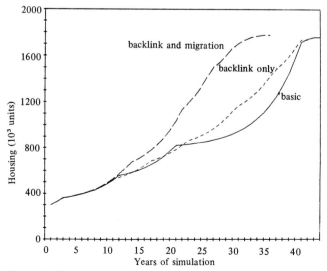

Figure 7. Illustrative output depicting structural intervention.

(UEL) scenario frees over 2500 acres of land for residential development at ten units per acre. This is a policy that the provincial government has been contemplating. This large tract of land is located next to a region of predominantly single-family dwellings, which are much in demand. The same figures also show the basic unconstrained run, a 'land act' run in which an agricultural land freeze is in effect, and a 'grand unzoning' in which much of the city is upzoned to higher-density housing and multifamily dwellings.

The distinction between upzoning and land-freezing policy is made clear in figure 8, which shows the effect of an UEL scenario for the total housing units in West Point Grey, and an upzoning scenario for the West End, the high-rise section of the city. Freeing land allows new development to take place, mere upzoning is restricted by the fact that there are already buildings present, and demolition occurs only on initially substandard properties. A fault of the model is that there is no aging process to allow redevelopment of depreciated properties. This is necessitated by the absence of any age-distribution data for the standing stock of buildings. In either case there is a ceiling which, once reached, precludes further development without freeing more land in some way. Removal and renewal of standing stock can be read in interactively as policies. As noted earlier, however, they are not accounted for in the dynamics of the present model.

Refinements currently under way include the estimation of housing supply and a dynamic demolition algorithm which systematically removes housing in upzoned areas. The supply equation is disaggregated into single

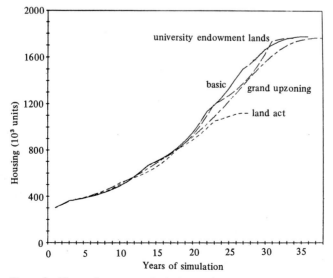

Figure 8. Illustrative output depicting qualitative intervention.

family/row housing and multiple-family housing and relates new construction to previous period starts by type, and previous and current population. These equations have been estimated and are currently being tested (January 1976). The demolition algorithms are being developed so that in cases of upzoning the existing lower-density stock can be removed over time to make way for higher-density (and higher-rent-paying) structures. This refinement is also running and being tested now. Finally additional land-use and employment data are being gathered to update and estimate a number of other algorithms which previously depended upon *ad hoc* assumptions for their operation. This is a longer-run task which will not be finished in the foreseeable future. The data base is also being disaggregated into 181 subareas.

4 Some general comments and speculative conclusions

In the first parts of this paper I set out some of the strategic and substantive questions that we addressed in our modelling efforts. In this final section I want to focus on a number of points which relate to the utility of simulation modelling, including some speculations concerning its likely role in decisionmaking and planning in the future. Accordingly below we will examine some conditions under which modelling is likely to survive and perhaps even prosper. Then I should like to explore the greatest danger of modelling, namely what happens if it is successful and widely used. We conclude by noting the importance of gaining experience in the use of models.

There are two broad sets of benefits that simulation models can yield. These benefits can derive from other technologies as well, so they are not the exclusive purview of simulation modelling. Such models (and impact assessing technologies in general) will be useful if they:
(a) provide more and/or better information than would otherwise be available,
(b) promote a flexible open-ended planning/decisionmaking process.
The first of these benefits is substantive and relates to the output from the modelling exercise, whereas the second is procedural and is independent of the quality of output, the process being itself an output.
Models can enhance the information base for decisions in two ways:
1. They can provide more information than was previously possible. This additional information can take the form of increased accuracy of existing information or new data items.
2. They can provide a framework for examining both old and new data in such a way that the real world phenomenon being modelled is more understandable. In this way they can provide access to information not previously accessible. Increased access to planning information is surely one of the most underrated values of simulation modelling (see Goldberg, 1974).

Turning to the procedural benefits that can derive from simulation modelling methodologies three advantages come to mind:

(1) Developing better *models* that evolve as the result of widespread use, criticism, and refinement. Such models will be designed to serve a variety of masters and purposes and thus enhance information flows.

(2) Developing a *model-building process* that is responsive to the needs of decisionmakers, technicians, and citizens. Whereas in the preceding item we were concerned with better models, here we are concerned with a more relevant and therefore usable model-building process that transcends the specifics of any given model.

(3) Building on the foregoing ideas, ultimately the extension of this process orientation takes us to the level of *planning and decisionmaking processes* in general. If we are faithful to the spirit of open-ended model-building processes, this same spirit will come to infuse decision-making processes. By being equally concerned for the processes which lead to decisions and for the substance of these decisions, societies evolve an approach to the unknown, since carefully evolved and modified processes are general in nature and therefore endure for centuries. The common law is such a process. Specific decisions arrived at through the application of these processes are usually much shorter-lived because of their specificity. A mix of the general (the process) and the specific (the decision's substance) is essential to allow the decisionmaking unit to survive the short-run (through the individual decision) to enable it to persevere in the longer run (through the application of a viable process) (Goldberg, 1975).

The foregoing discussion of processes versus products is not new but has been the focus of numerous soul-searching and soul-justifying exercises in the planning and decisionmaking literature. I want to turn now, however, to a much overlooked phenomenon which is one of the most destructive institutions developed to date by western culture. It is the undoing of both products and processes. It is the institution of 'success'.

There are numerous examples of ideas, programmes, products, and processes that began with the highest intentions and over time have become institutionalized and self-serving. The welfare system in the United States is an example of a noble idea which when transformed into a programme became institutionalized so that its success is not measured by its ability to eliminate poverty or raise people's standard of living, but rather by the number of people on welfare rolls. More welfare recipients is equated with success, which is clearly fallacious. The automobile and petroleum industries represent purveyors of products that have become so central to the North American way of life that their perpetuation is taken for granted and is independent of the social costs. In each case socially beneficial ideas, products, or services have been subverted through their widespread adoption (that is, success). Two contrasting examples come to mind.

The Tennessee Valley Authority (TVA) was one of many innovative agencies founded during the Great Depression. TVA was a regional agency whose authority crossed a number of state boundaries. Initially TVA was really an environmental protection agency responsible for the Tennessee Valley region. As a joint product of flood control efforts came hydroelectricity generation. Electricity turned out to be the central product that TVA produced.

Power generation grew in importance and environmental protection waned. When I visited Oak Ridge in 1971 more than 92% of TVA electricity was generated by thermal plants (predominantly coal fired) and less than 8% came from hydroelectric generators. For roughly forty years TVA fought for its survival in a region that despised federal intervention. It succeeded and today is one of the major users of strip-mined coal and thus is responsible for a large amount of the environmental degradation caused by strip mining each year in the TVA region. From environmental protector to environmental destroyer in less than two generations. That's the power of success.

The Montaignais-Naskapi Indians deal with the problem differently. Wary of overcropping the caribou herds upon which their survival hinged historically, these people regulated hunting through the ritual use of a caribou scapula for divination. Each year a scapula was heated, and as a result cracks were formed as it dried. The shaman instructed hunters in how to read these cracks as a map. Using this 'map', hunters set out to find the caribou each year. Using a different 'map' each year had the effect of randomizing the hunt and therefore spreading it over different caribou herds, thus allowing each herd a period of years to recoup its numbers.

Numerous examples exist of such risk avoidance and success-mitigating behaviour practices among the aboriginal peoples of the world (see Vadya, 1969). These people could not afford the mistakes of becoming dependent upon technology and allowing it to rule their lives. Ritual regulation of their actions provided protection against technological successes on a variety of fronts. I am not advocating a 'return to nature', but rather illustrating the need for success-moderating behaviour.

How does the foregoing relate to simulation models? In the past, models have not been overwhelmingly successful. As a result they have not gained widespread credibility and use. There are indications that this is changing, and certainly if we continue to improve our models they will become more widely accepted (Pack, 1975). The danger exists for successes to become institutionalized as they have elsewhere in western societies and thus get out of reach of the technicians who developed them or the society for which they were ostensibly designed. We should try to avoid what I have termed the 'oracular danger' wherein models are looked upon as oracles that provide genuine deity-certified truth. The certification deity in this case is computer and planning technology. Just as oracles in

ancient Greece often degenerated into means for legitimizing decisions that
had previously been taken, similar fates await models that are not process-
oriented, transparent, and widely accessible. The weaknesses of models
should be stressed before one boasts of their virtues. Caution should be
preached before blind faith and acceptance.

In model building, as in planning on the whole, there is a significant
need for a fusion of product and process. Substance and form should
complement each other, not be mutually exclusive. IIPS overcame the
weaknesses of earlier work I had done (Center for Real Estate and Urban
Economics, 1968) by focussing on process over product (the model). IIPS
can be typified as an exercise in process and form with unfortunately little
substance.

What is needed is a synthetic approach that merges both the product
and process orientations into one. I feel that the model-building process
set out at the beginning of this paper provides a framework within which
such a synthesis could occur. Such a synthesis must be built on experience
in building models, listening to criticisms about them, and refining them in
light of these experiences and criticisms. "Often, correct knowledge can
be arrived at only after many repetitions of the process leading from
matter to consciousness and then back to matter, that is, leading from
practice to knowledge and then back to practice" (Mao Tsetung, 1972,
pages 208–209).

By honouring both well-constructed models and well-thought-out and
flexible processes, we should be able to build both better models and
better processes. Better decisions should result. Information is the
essential output of modelling. Better and more responsive models and
model-building processes should provide more and better information.
Information is a fuel for decisionmaking, and models have a key role to
play. They must be widely accessible and relevant, however. If models
can meet tests of relevance, accessibility, and transparency, they will likely
prosper and provide a much needed input to our pluralistic society:
information and education.

"And say, finally, whether peace is best preserved by giving energy to the
government, or information to the people. This last is the most certain,
and the most legitimate engine of government. Educate and inform the
whole mass of the people. Enable them to see that it is in their interest
to preserve peace and order, and they will preserve them. And it requires
no very high degree of education to convince them of this. They are the
only sure reliance for the preservation of our liberty" (Thomas Jefferson,
1787, quoted in Padover, 1939, page 23).

References

Center for Real Estate and Urban Economics, 1968 *Jobs, People and Land: The Bay
    Area Simulation Study* Center for Real Estate and Urban Economics, University of
    California, Berkeley

Goldberg M A, 1968 "Bay Area simulation study: employment location models" *The Annals of Regional Science* **2** 161-176

Goldberg M A, 1973 "Simulation, synthesis and urban public decision-making" *Management Science* **20** Part II, 629-643

Goldberg M A, 1974 "Environmental decision-making: social indicators, simulation and public choice" *The Annals of Regional Science* **8** 12-23

Goldberg M A, 1975 "On the inefficiency of being efficient" *Environment and Planning A* **7** 921-939

Goldberg M A, Ash D A, "Simulation, information and interactive graphics: implications for public participation programs" *Transportation Research Record* forthcoming

Goldberg M A, Holling C S, 1970 "The Vancouver regional inter-institutional policy simulator" Resource Science Centre, University of British Columbia, Vancouver (mimeo)

Goldberg M A, Stander J M, "The modelbuilding process: analysis of output and policy application of an urban simulation model" *Transportation Research Record* forthcoming

Lee D B Jr, 1973 "Requiem for large-scale models" *Journal of the American Institute of Planners* **39** 163-178

Mao Tsetung, 1972 *Quotations from Chairman Mao Tsetung* (Foreign Language Press, Peking)

Milsum J, Uyeno D, Vertinsky I, 1971 "Vancouver regional health planning model" Institute of Animal Resource Ecology, University of British Columbia, Vancouver (mimeo)

Pack J R, 1975 "The use of urban models: report on survey of planning organizations" *Journal of the American Institute of Planners* **41** 191-199

Padover S K (Ed.), 1939 *Thomas Jefferson on Democracy* (Mentor Books, New York)

Putman S H, 1972 "Intraurban employment forecasting models: a review and a suggested new model construct" *Journal of the American Institute of Planners* **38** 216-230

Swoveland D, Uyeno D, Vertinsky I, Vickson R, 1973 "Ambulance location: A probabilistic enumeration approach" *Management Science* **20** Part II, 686-698

Vayda A P (Ed.), 1969 *Environment and Cultural Behavior* (Natural History Press, New York)

Spatial Externalities and Locational Conflict

M.DEAR
McMaster University

Introduction
The location of controversial public facilities is often associated with a
wide range of community opposition. Much of the ensuing locational
conflict is caused by individuals or groups who are concerned neither with
the function of the facility, nor with consuming the good or service which
is its output. For example, neighbourhood opposition is typically based
upon objection to the noise of a proposed facility or to its effect on local
property values. Such opposition occurs in response to the facility's
external effects; it generally has little to do with the functioning or
service of the facility *per se.*

The incidence of external effects and the concomitant locational
conflict pose considerable problems for the location theorist and planner.
Because of the *public* nature of the decision process, the incidence of
external costs and benefits has to be incorporated into the locational
calculus. The external effects cannot be ignored by decisionmakers. Very
often for instance the impacted community group has to be compensated
for the negative effects of a facility's location. Moreover the blocking of
a preferred location may seriously imbalance the spatial configuration of
the facility set.

Until very recently the problem of externalities and conflict has been
ignored in location theory. Analysts have tended to regard public-facility
location as a special case of commercial or retail location, or as something
predetermined by residential development in the private sector. However,
it has become increasingly evident that such approaches are severely
limited if one attempts to explain either the *process* or the *impact* of
locational decisions.

In order to illustrate this fundamental criticism let us briefly consider
the significance of the process and impact dimensions in public facility
location. Some years ago a decision was made to locate a drug
treatment centre in the Germantown area of north Philadelphia. Several
neighbourhood groups protested against the decision. The strongest
dissent was associated with a gang of black teenagers, who claimed that
the proposed centre was a white, middle-class 'rip-off'. A second group
opposed any centre in their community because they felt there already
were too many public facilities there. A third group was against the
specific site which was proposed, since it was close to a local school and
they feared the children would be introduced to the drug subculture.

In contrast, the proposed centre was supported by a loose coalition of
local politicians and residents who were concerned about the obvious drug

problem in the area. Feelings on all sides became so intense that the City of Philadelphia agreed to hold a public meeting at which a binding vote would be taken for or against the centre. Not surprisingly the opposition groups arranged for the meeting to be packed by their sympathisers. At the end of a noisy meeting, the proposal for a drug treatment centre was overwhelmingly rejected, and the City began its search for an alternative location.

Notice the following characteristics of this situation:
a) The traditional concerns of optimality and efficiency in location, and of rational decisionmaking, are all rendered redundant, since the City was pressured into delegating decisionmaking authority to an unspecified constituency at a single public meeting convened especially for that purpose.
b) Community antagonism to the proposed centre was entirely founded in opposition to the external effects of the facility, although the precise motive for opposition varied among the three groups.
c) The City misjudged the degree of community opposition to the proposed centre. Yet its perceived negative impact generated sufficient opposition to force the City to abandon its original plan.

Effective planning for public-facility location clearly requires a location theory which can account for locational process as well as locational impact, which provides a central focus upon the impact of external effects in particular, and which incorporates the political dimensions of public decisionmaking. This paper therefore attempts to relate the two fundamental concepts of spatial externalities and locational conflict in some systematic manner, in order to provide a framework for understanding location decisions in the public sector. The two concepts are initially explored separately, but then are brought together in an examination of mental-health-facility location. Finally the lessons of this evidence are drawn together to suggest some new directions for a location theory of the public sector.

Spatial externalities
External effects
It may be useful to begin by briefly reviewing the traditional approach to the analysis of externalities; in this manner the conventions later utilized in this paper may be less ambiguous. Externalities (external effects, spillovers) are normally regarded as the unpriced effects of a certain activity upon groups or individuals who are not directly involved in that activity. Such effects can arise from a wide range of sources (Hill, 1973, chapter 1), although all can be resolved into the general case of the failure of markets to exist. The problem of market failure has caused major problems in the theoretical literature (Staaf and Tannian, 1973). A commonly advocated solution suggests the adoption of a system of taxes or subsidies to control externalities. The tax on any particular activity would equal the marginal 'social damage' which it generates. Another

approach has been to search for the weakest set of conditions which
would ensure that a Pareto-type efficient, competitive equilibrium exists
when externalities are present (Arrow, 1970).

From a more practical viewpoint the 'standards and prices' approach to
the control of external effects has gained wide approval. This involves the
selection of a set of arbitrary standards for the environment and the
calculation of a set of prices sufficient to attain these standards (Baumol
and Oates, 1971). In contrast to the theoretical solutions described in the
preceding paragraph, the standards and prices approach recognizes that
external effects cannot adequately be controlled solely within the price
system.

It is only since analysts have ceased trying to internalize externalities
that their full significance is being realized. Mishan (1969) for example
has argued that the incidence and significance of external effects increase
as societies grow in material wealth. As a consequence greater emphasis
has recently been laid on control mechanisms which are outside the price
system, such as legal and administrative regulations (Davis and Kamien,
1970). In short it is becoming increasingly evident that traditional criteria
for analyzing externalities have considerable shortcomings. Alexander
(1970) concludes bluntly that an understanding of the external impact of
urban decisions requires a model much more complex than the existing
competitive equilibrium models.

Spatial external effects
It is a simple task to incorporate a spatial dimension into the notion of
external effects. The typical case of 'geographic spillovers' occurs in
education when a person educated at the expense of taxpayers migrates to
another jurisdiction, thus transferring the benefits of the education to a
separate group of taxpayers (Weisbrod, 1965). A simpler and more
common case is that in which any external effect is constrained to a
spatially limited area. For example if pedestrian–vehicle accidents are
regarded as an external effect of highway operation, the spatial extent of
that effect is necessarily confined to the vicinity of the highway.

Externalities may therefore be regarded as having a spatially limited
'field' of effects. These externality fields define the limits of the geographic
spillover effect (Harvey, 1973, chapter 2). The extent and configuration
of the externality field will be influenced by several variables, including
the size and type of the externality source, and the nature and density of
the surrounding properties. This latter factor is particularly important,
since the advantages (or disadvantages) associated with a facility's location
do not necessarily accrue equally among all properties. Instead there tends
to be a systematic decline in the external effect over distance as proximity
to its source diminishes. Such a distance-decay effect has been observed
empirically in many cases, as for example in the case of urban parks
(Hammer et al., 1971) and urban renewal projects (Rothenburg, 1967).

Note that this effect depends heavily upon the crucial assumption that the land and/or property market can discriminate spatially by bidding up (or down) values within the externality field just equal to the variable incidence of the external effect.

The discriminatory capacity of the market depends itself upon the perception of, or attitudes of property owners toward, the facility in question. In order to illustrate the potential impact of variable perceptions, consider the example of urban parkland location. Granting that the park will tend to increase property values in its vicinity, let us consider the precise nature of that increase, as manifest in the distance-decay profile of the park's externality field (figure 1). Three kinds of property-owner response may be suggested:

a) Property owners are homogeneous in their perception of parkland spillovers, and the external effect is purely a function of proximity to the park. In this case the distance-decay profile of the externality field will have a linear form (QQ'). The spatial limit of the externality field is given by the distance OS, and the aggregate location rent which may be ascribed to the presence of the park is given by the area PQQ'.

b) Property owners are extremely sensitive to distance, and external effects are consequently intensely concentrated in the immediate vicinity of the park. However, this effect diminishes rapidly over distance. In this instance, an exponential profile (RR') might be expected.

c) Property owners have mixed reactions. Those in close proximity to the park suffer from the noise and inconvenience of its visitors, and this negative impact offsets any property value gain. However, those further from the park are increasingly insulated from the nuisance of visitors, and

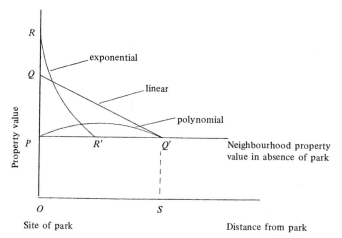

Figure 1. Variation in externality-field profile according to property owners' perceptions.

their property values appreciated to some maximum value, thereafter declining 'normally' with distance. In this final example, the externality field might have a polynomial profile (PQ').

Externality-field analysis

The analysis of externality fields as a source of locational conflict is a difficult task. Before discussing the analytical problems specifically, it is worthwhile recalling that external effects in this context refer to any facility impacts which are not directly related to consumption of the good or service which is output from that facility. It is important to emphasize that both consumers (users) and nonconsumers (nonusers) of the facility may benefit or suffer from external effects. For present purposes these categories may be conveniently designated respectively as user-associated and neighbourhood-associated external effects. The distinction between the user and neighbourhood components of a facility's externality field is important in understanding many conflict situations.

The case of user-associated externalities is the more complex. Two specific classes may be recognized: personal and exogenous. The consumption of certain goods may cause a reaction in the user; this is understood to define a 'personal user externality'. For example there is a certain stigma attached to welfare payments or residence in public housing. In addition users may suffer from the nuisance of other users or of queuing to obtain service. On the positive side, users may enjoy the company and help of other users at a facility. The incidence of such personal external effects can have a significant impact on user attitude and utilization.

When a user is affected by externalities, but the source of the external effects lies outside the individual, they are termed 'exogenous user externalities'. Thus a user will benefit if all internal scale economies have been captured in the facility's operation. Or else urbanization and localization economies may enable the user to take advantage of situations of choice, or multiple-purpose visits. Clearly this separate category of user-associated externalities is related to the traditional concept of agglomeration economies. However, the emphasis here is upon the benefits to the *client*, not those of the facility or operator.

Neighbourhood-associated externalities simply refer to those cases where a facility's external effects have an impact upon the utility of a nonuser. It includes such considerations as the problem of noise and air pollution from industrial operations, or the spillover effects from urban renewal. Nonuser perceptions of these externalities determine the extent and intensity of neighbourhood antagonism toward a particular facility or service.

User- and neighbourhood-associated external effects are often extremely difficult to analyze. Most of the analytical difficulties are related to the problem of measurement. One of the most difficult tasks, for example, is defining the relevant impact area for any external effect. A too narrowly defined area involves underestimating a facility's impact, while too broad an area risks diluting it. There is also the problem of 'noise' in measuring external effects. One is never certain that the effects being observed can be attributed to the facility being studied. For instance, some distant change in a transportation system may induce an accessibility-related change in property values which could 'drown' the effect of any public facility. Even in a relatively straightforward analysis of property values, Schall (1971) has pointed out that the value of land and the value of the structure upon it can often move in different directions. The resultant impact therefore depends upon the relative magnitude of these two discrete changes.

The core of the problem of externality-field analysis lies in the fact that we are concerned with the *net* impact of that field. For example in figure 1 it was suggested (in the case of the polynomial profile) that the nuisance effect of close proximity to the park cancelled out any potential gain in property value. In this case the park has two externality fields: one positive, representing an increase in property value; one negative, a nuisance effect which offsets the property value effect. Moreover these two externality fields have *coalesced* to produce an external effect significantly different from the simple effect of the two fields taken separately. Nonuser attitudes toward the park will clearly be determined in this instance by the net effect of the two externality fields.

The coalescence of two external effects from one facility is less common than the coalescence of single fields from a large number of facilities. Such coalescence is implicit in the existence of suburbanization and localization economies associated with multiple-facility complexes. The analytical problem faced in this instance involves disaggregating for the source of each effect, then aggregating to assess the net impact.

Locational conflict
Locational conflict may be defined as overt public debate over some actual or proposed land use or property development. This debate can take several forms, including public discussion, referendum, or demonstration. The conflict paradigm is a relatively new approach to spatial problems and reflects (at least in part) a dissatisfaction with the classical market models which are traditionally used to examine the resolution of conflicting pressures for land-use change. The emphasis in locational conflict is upon decisions—the processes by which they are made, and the impact they have. Of course the literature on decision theory is extremely rich; however, it is also largely aspatial. Only more recently have spatial studies of conflict been appearing (Cox, 1973; Harvey, 1973; Isard et al., 1969; and Wolpert et al., 1972).

The unique circumstances under which each conflict occurs have caused most conflict analysts to proceed on a case-by-case basis. Each problem is regarded as an independent event, with different actors, issues, and outcomes. The major drawback in this case-study approach is that it becomes exceedingly difficult to recognize the system-wide impacts of a specific decision and to make comparative analyses across a set of case studies. A formal theory of locational conflict is thus slow to appear.

For the moment there is no simple answer to this aggregation problem. However, Seley (1973) has suggested that it may be possible to determine the major structural *dimensions* of a sample of conflict situations. These define the major variables and parameters which consistently recur in any locational conflict. For the problem of conflict over public-facility location, we may recognize two fundamental dimensions. These relate to the facility itself (its *form*) and the nature of the host community (its *context*). In many ways therefore the public-facility location problem can be conceived as an exercise in design, the object of which is to achieve 'goodness of fit' between form and context (cf Alexander, 1964). Where fit is poor, conflict may be anticipated.

In what follows, the dimensions of form and context are examined more closely to determine the facility and community 'impact variables'. Taken together, these define what appear to be the most important structural elements in conflict over the external effects associated with public facility location. As such, they provide a systematic (if not fully rigorous) framework for the analysis of that conflict.

Form: facility impact variables

The impact of a particular facility appears to be determined by three specific dimensions: scale, type, and degree of noxiousness. Needless to say, all three are closely interrelated.

The *scale* of a facility is an obvious concern in conflict analysis, since *ceteris paribus* it may be assumed that the larger its scale, the larger its impact and the greater the likelihood that it will generate opposition. Thus a row house used as a residence for runaway adolescents is a potentially less disruptive influence than the siting of a power plant. It is possible for the scale dimension to be compounded by the number of facilities in a neighbourhood. Here the scale of the multiple-facility complex becomes the important variable (cf the coalescence discussion in the preceding section).

Along the *type* dimension a fundamental distinction may be made between a service-type facility, and a despatch- or depot-type facility. In the case of the former, clients travel to the facility in order to consume the good (as for example to a library). In the case of the latter, goods are taken to the client for consumption (as in the case of most emergency services). A third category recognizes the 'network' characteristics of most public-utility operations, like electricity, sewage, etc (Teitz, 1968). All three types of facility have different operating characteristics, and it seems likely that each will generate a different range of external effects. For example the nuisance of visiting clients may be the biggest external effect of a service facility; the constant exit of emergency vehicles, that of a despatch facility; and the disruption of repair and maintenance crews, that of a utility facility.

The third component of facility form is its *degree of noxiousness*. This dimension is usefully distinguished from the simple physical measures of scale and type, since it begins to provide a behavioural explanation of community perceptions and attitudes toward facility externality fields. Many public facilities appear to be regarded as 'noxious' in the sense that they are clearly perceived as needed within a particular neighbourhood, but they are not necessarily desired by the residents in proximity to any potential site (Austin et al., 1970). In understanding community opposition, it is necessary to recognize which components of the facility itself generate the noxiousness reaction.

Context: community impact variables

The response to a particular facility is determined by three community impact variables, which together define the context for the form in question. These three variables are socioeconomic status, strategy, and motivation.

Socioeconomic status refers to the range of demographic, social, and economic characteristics of the host community. These characteristics determine the propensity of any neighbourhood group to become involved in a conflict situation. This 'propensity to participate' is not reflected in any simple relationship with socioeconomic status, but there is a tendency for certain groups to become involved in conflict more than others. Hence, the small, organized, middle-income group is generally involved more frequently and more effectively than the large, loosely knit, low-income group (Olson, 1971).

At the same time, the socioeconomic characteristics of any neighbourhood provide guidance on the likely potential impact of a new facility. For instance, a drug treatment centre might have a high impact in a relatively homogeneous, single-family residential neighbourhood. However, the same centre might go unnoticed in an obsolescent, inner-city area of mixed land uses, and transient population.

The more effective participation of a middle-income group clearly reflects the distribution of power in the political system. Although the power variable is intrinsically interesting in its own right, we are more concerned here with the effect it has on the various *strategies* which are available to the impacted groups, since not all strategies will be available to every group continuously. Three important options may be noticed: exit, voice, and violence (figure 2). Exit may be interpreted as ceasing to consume one good in favour of another. In public-goods terms, this implies 'voting with the feet' in search of a government jurisdiction in which the public-goods package better matches consumer preference (cf Tiebout, 1956). Voice, on the other hand, is the strategy of the group which remains *in situ* and sues for improvement in the quality of a good via the political process. This latter option is clearly of major significance in public decision processes. The exit–voice dichotomy is explored by Hirschman (1970). Williams (1971) has noted the distinction between voice strategies by coalition, and by community. The former refers to an alliance of diverse socioeconomic groups with a simple common interest, say, to stop an airport expansion. The latter refers to an opposition group which is homogeneous in some important characteristic (race, for example). A coalition exists only while the common interest persists; in contrast the community has an existence independent of a specific conflict.

A third strategy, violence, includes any illegal action or threat of illegal action, such as riot, damage to property, etc. These aggressive responses are not necessarily the last resort of a community group, but may be used selectively prior to the adoption of another strategy. (All three strategies noted here may be used in combination or in sequence, according to the characteristics of the group involved.) The *threat* of violence is itself an effective strategy.

The third community impact variable is *motivation*. Clearly the precise reason for individual or group involvement in any locational conflict will be complex. Williams (1971) refers to the rather nebulous concept of 'dissatisfaction'. Williamson (1970) analyzes the 'demoralization costs' attributable to the 'capricious redistributions' which derive from external effects. However, greater precision is introduced by Gurr (1970), who has examined 'relative deprivation' as a source of public violence. Relative

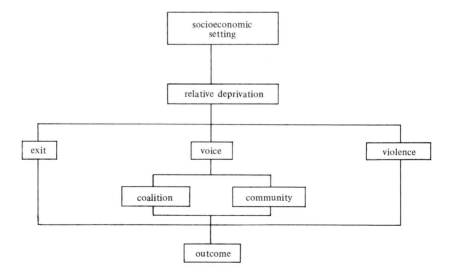

Figure 2. Relationship amongst the community impact variables.

deprivation measures the gap between what one feels one deserves and what one is actually capable of getting (and retaining). In conflict terms, the gap is measured in relation to the distributive impact of the potential land-use development. The greater the dissatisfaction with the distributive consequences, the greater will be the propensity to participate in conflict (figure 2).

Absence of fit and the generation of conflict

Locational conflict can be viewed as the result of the absence of 'fit' between the facility and community impact variables. The attitude of the host community toward a facility will clearly depend upon the attributes of that facility, as summarized in the scale, type, and noxiousness dimensions. The community response will, however, be simultaneously conditioned by its internal characteristics (socioeconomic status, available strategies, and motivation), which together define its propensity to participate in the conflict.

The systematic study of these six interdependent dimensions will hopefully explain much about the generation and process of locational conflict. What we shall look for in the subsequent empirical analysis is conflict and bargaining over the distributive consequences of the positive and negative externality fields of various public facilities. Where these fields coalesce, and both positive and negative effects are present, their *net* impact will be of interest. Our explanation ought then to focus on how these opposite effects are *traded off* in the community's 'mind' to produce the net impact. In the case of the urban park, for example, the negative nuisance value of visitors just offsets the positive property-value effect of the park itself. A rather more complex trade-off might involve evaluating the positive 'psychic benefit' of helping local drug addicts against the negative cost of fear for one's personal security. If direct consumption-related variables are allowed to enter the reckoning, an even more complex trade-off must occur. Here a balance between the benefits of consumption and the costs of any external effects may be observed. For example a police station may be regarded as a noisy neighbour, but such external costs are far outweighed by the consumption-related security benefits which accrue to the host community.

Conflict over mental health facility location

The federally funded programme for community mental health centres was begun in the United States during the late 1960s. Its intention was to decentralize mental health care into neighbourhood-based 'satellite' facilities. For the purposes of this paper it will be sufficient to examine one out of many locational problems associated with the community mental health programme. This is the tendency for group homes for former mental hospital patients to become spatially concentrated in inner-city residential areas. It is a phenomenon which has been observed in

many US cities, including San Francisco, New York, and Philadelphia
(Dear, 1974b). It has developed because health planners, faced with
considerable opposition in many neighbourhoods, have reacted by seeking
out potential locations where little opposition may be anticipated. These
include the relatively obsolete areas of downtown with many transient
rooming-houses, or commercial/industrial areas where no zoning variance is
required (Wolpert et al., 1975).

Form

Group homes for former mental hospital patients are normally converted
residential structures, varying in size from a small row house to a larger
detached dwelling capable of housing up to twenty people. In the latter
case the houses may effectively be regarded as boarding homes, or small
hotels. They are, however, essentially small-scale structures, and one
would anticipate that their potential impact would be minor.

The homes function as residences for the ex-patients. They are service-
type facilities insofar as they oblige clients to come to them for service.
In fact they may cause a relatively high level of activity, since residents
make frequent 'visits' to their home.

Group homes appear to be associated with a high degree of noxiousness,
especially when a large number of the residents are so-called 'chronic'
patients. These people tend to display certain aberrant behavioural
characteristics, which in turn makes them highly visible in a 'normal'
community. Consequently they are highly newsworthy, and some of the
events described below took place against a backdrop of sensationalist
journalism, which focused upon such wild behaviour as urinating in public,
or drinking beer and watching television all day!

From our viewpoint the outstanding characteristic of the group-home-
ghetto phenomenon is that it represents an extreme case of externality-field
coalescence. The potential impact of what are predominantly small-scale,
low-activity centres is therefore significantly compounded by a *multiple-
facility impact*. For example the town of Long Beach, Long Island, has
2500 of the 3500 licensed beds for released patients in the whole of
Nassau County, as well as 500 unlicensed beds. In California the San Jose
neighbourhood has 74% of Santa Clara County's bedspaces, housing 2000
ex-patients in an area of 20000 residents. Similar trends have been
observed in Canada (Murphy et al., 1972); in addition Titmuss (1965) has
noted that community-care hostels in Britain tend to 'silt up' with the
chronically mentally ill.

Context

The respective contexts for conflict over group-home location in Long Beach
and San Jose are quite different. Long Beach is a prosperous town on
Long Island. It is relatively homogeneous and stable in population terms,
functioning mainly as a dormitory and vacation centre for New Yorkers.

The San Jose area is older, and was dominated by university student accommodation prior to the influx of former patients. It is a rather run-down neighbourhood, with a predominantly transient population which includes students, faculty, landlords, retailers, and families.

In terms of the respective socioeconomic settings, the potential impact of the community mental health programme could not be unambiguously predicted. For instance could one expect tolerance or opposition from the relatively 'conservative' residents of Long Beach? Or would the 'liberal' melting pot in San Jose show greater tolerance? In order to explain what the actual responses were, it is useful to examine another variable in the context dimension—the motivations of the various participant groups.

From the viewpoint of the ex-patient the 'ghettoization' of group homes has much to offer in terms of user-associated externalities. It provides a supportive environment, and individual civil rights are better protected. The San Jose community has for example a local newspaper, and the ex-patients help each other in many daily ways to cope with their new situation. A wide range of support services, such as a job referral centre, have also been located within the community.

The range of supportive user-associated externalities associated with the coalescence of the group-home externality fields is suggested by table 1. In this matrix a positive (beneficial) association between the two facilities is noted thus (+), as for example in the case of two group homes. Similarly there will be a positive relationship between group home and job referral centre. The matrix can be extended to indicate negative (−) and neutral (0) associations. Thus the operations of community mental health centre and methadone maintenance programmes appear to conflict (Coughlan et al., 1974), whereas Russo (1974) has documented the mutually therapeutic interaction between mental patients and delinquents.

Table 1. Matrix of interdependencies among five types of mental health facilities.

	Group home	Job referral	Community mental health centre	Methadone maintenance	Delinquency
Group home	+[a]				
Job referral	+	+			
Community mental health centre	0[b]	+	+		
Methadone maintenance	0	+	−[c]	+	
Delinquency	0	+	+	0	+

[a] positive (beneficial) reinforcement
[b] neutral
[c] negative (harmful) reinforcement

Presumably those associations only exist while the facilities are close
enough for their externality fields to overlap. If the distance between two
facilities is increased to the point when the fields no longer coalesce, then
any positive or negative association will be neutralized.

From a user viewpoint there is a strong motivation to continue the
existence of the group-home ghettos. However, from a neighbourhood
viewpoint the coalescence issue is seen somewhat differently. The
coalescence of group-home externality fields is perceived by nonusers as a
'saturation' effect. A kind of 'institutional tipping' has occurred, translating
what was once an area of residential land uses into one of predominantly
institutional uses (Dear, 1974a). In general the highly negative impact of
the neighbourhood-associated externalities seems to revolve around the
issue of the destruction of community. In Long Beach for example the
influx of former patients has presented a choice between the "health of
the community, and the health of the patients" (Dear, 1974b, chapter 5).
The not untypical concern with a possible decline in property values was
also evident.

In summary the ghetto 'form' that has evolved seems beneficial to users,
but it has not been sympathetically received in the neighbourhood
'context' where it evolved. The absence of fit between form and context
generated intense conflict in both our sample communities.

Conflict outcome
The residents of the group homes tend not to enter into conflict over the
impact of the homes. Instead their case is argued by a surrogate—namely,
the administration responsible for their placement in the community. This
is because the group as a whole lack the experience and skills to represent
themselves. (In a separate Californian situation the threat to terminate the
hospital patient release programme was sufficient to galvanize both
ex-patients and their advocates to fight for its continuation.)

The nonuser group in contrast has the full range of conflict strategies
available to it (figure 2). In San Jose the predominantly student and
working-class community changed rapidly as the student population exited
and was replaced by ex-patients (in a classic neighbourhood succession).
The anticipated decline in the neighbourhood did not occur; no loss of
property value was observed—thus replicating the results of a wider study
of property-value impacts of mental health facilities in Philadelphia (Dear,
1974b). However, the remaining residents began to voice their opposition
to the increasing proliferation of group homes in their area. Ultimately an
ordinance was passed preventing the establishment of more than one group
home per block. This can be regarded as a direct *concession* to the
neighbourhood in return for withdrawal of their opposition to the
programme.

Concessions are an important factor in many locational conflicts. They
are generally used during an arbitration process to appease an opposition

group. In another situation in Philadelphia the opposition of a small resident group (to a hospital outreach programme) was stifled by the building of a high screening wall which created an effective visual barrier between the residents and the outreach centre in their neighbourhood. The cost of this wall was $1500. The leaders of the opposition group were subsequently *co-opted* by the hospital administration, while the community as a whole *resigned* themselves to the continuing institutional tipping.

The situation in Long Beach was a little different. The long-term residents, predominantly middle-income property owners, quickly voiced a strong protest against the influx of ex-patients. There is little evidence of any exit on the part of residents, since the patients were predominantly taking up space in the many vacant spaces in small hotels in this vacation area. (The landlords prefer a steady, year-round income.) Again a local zoning ordinance was passed preventing any further influx of ex-patients into the community. This move was challenged on constitutional grounds, and the ensuing furore caused a statewide inquiry into the discharge of mental hospital patients. Recently the New York State Department of Mental Hygiene announced a policy to slow the release of mental patients from mental hospitals. Although in this paper we have only indirectly considered the strategies available to the public decision authority, it is pertinent to note that the health planners have here engaged in *nondecision-making*. This refers to any decision taken to suppress a challenge to the interests of the decisionmaker; it is an important strategy in the armoury of public decision authorities (Bachrach and Baratz, 1970, page 44).

In both Long Beach and San Jose the continued development of the community mental health programme has effectively been arrested. This has resulted from a politically expedient rush to minimize the negative impact of neighbourhood-associated external effects. The positive advantages of the externality fields for the user have been ignored. Hence in dismantling the ghetto a supportive environment unknowingly created for the user may be just as unwittingly destroyed.

Conclusion

Many unanswered questions remain in our study of group-home externality fields. A large number of these relate to the politics of public decision-making—for example what are the dynamics of the arbitration process in locational conflict? Obviously a large number of groups are co-opted by various concessions into accepting the political decision. But what happens to the groups which are defeated in a conflict? A severe fragmentation occurs in many instances; groups refuse, or are unable to recognize, a common interest and are effectively neutralized. This process of 'group fragmentation' is often compounded by a 'group internalization' where intragroup conflict leads to an internal reward–status activity (cf Ley, 1974).

Other relevant considerations which remain undeveloped in this paper include a study of the *institutional constraints* which define the structure of political decisionmaking. The important role of property rights in creating externalities and in guiding decisions has long been recognized for example, as well as the influence of government and jurisdictional organization on urban welfare (Cox and Dear, 1975). It also seems essential to define those *attributes* of public facilities which induce a positive or negative reaction in users and nonusers. We may talk for instance about cultural and administrative accessibility, as well as simple physical accessibility. The way in which these attributes are translated into community *attitudes* or perceptions might help us to define the trade-off (between negative and positive impacts) which is an important element of locational conflict (Dear and Fincher, 1975).

This paper has outlined a framework for the analysis of some of these important questions. The thrust of this research is away from traditional location theory, which tends to emphasize only the direct, consumption-related aspects of location. The central concern of this paper is the role of spatial external effects in locational conflict. Such concerns might be viewed as part of the new attempt at defining the geographical foundations of the urban political economy (see Harvey, 1973; Roweis, 1975; and Scott, 1975, for major efforts in this direction).

References
Alexander C, 1964 *Notes on the Synthesis of Form* (Harvard University Press, Cambridge, Mass.)
Alexander S S, 1970 "Comment" in *The Analysis of Public Output* Ed. J Margolis (National Bureau of Economic Research, New York)
Arrow K J, 1970 "Political and economic evaluation of social effects and externalities" in *The Analysis of Public Output* Ed. J Margolis (National Bureau of Economic Research, New York)
Austin M, Smith T E, Wolpert J, 1970 "The implementation of controversial facility-complex programs" *Geographical Analysis* **2** 315-329
Bachrach P, Baratz M S, 1970 *Power and Poverty* (Oxford University Press, New York)
Baumol W J, Oates W E, 1971 "The uses of standards and prices for protection of the environment" *Swedish Journal of Economics* **73** 42-54
Coughlan A J, Pixley L, Zimmerman R S, 1974 "Community mental health concepts and methadone maintenance: Are they compatible?" *Community Mental Health Journal* **10** 426-433
Cox K R, 1973 *Conflict, Power, and Politics in the City* (McGraw-Hill, New York)
Cox K R, Dear M, 1975 "Jurisdictional organization and urban welfare" DP 47, Department of Geography, Ohio State University, Columbus
Davis O A, Kamien M I, 1970 "Externalities, information, and alternative collective action" in *Public Expenditures and Policy Analysis* Eds R H Haveman, J Margolis (Markham, Chicago)
Dear M, 1974a "A paradigm for public facility location theory" *Antipode* **6** 46-50 [Reprinted in Gale S, Moore E, 1975 *The Manipulated City* (Maaroufa Press, Chicago)]
Dear M, 1974b *Locational Analysis for Public Mental Health Facilities* unpublished Ph D dissertation, University of Pennsylvania, Philadelphia
Dear M, Fincher R, 1975 "The external effects of public programs" paper presented at the 22nd Annual Meeting of the Regional Science Association, Cambridge, Mass.
Gurr T R, 1970 *Why Men Rebel* (Princeton University Press, Princeton, NJ)

Hammer T R, Horn E, Coughlin R E, 1971 "The effect of a large urban park on real estate value" DP 51, Regional Science Research Institute, Philadelphia, Pa

Harvey D, 1973 *Social Justice and the City* (Edward Arnold, London)

Hill M, 1973 *Planning for Multiple Objectives* Monograph Series number 5, Regional Science Research Institute, Philadelphia, Pa

Hirschman A O, 1970 *Exit, Voice, and Loyalty* (Harvard University Press, Cambridge, Mass.)

Isard W, Smith T E, Isard P, Tung T H, Dacey M, 1969 *General Theory: Social, Political, Economic and Regional* (MIT Press, Cambridge, Mass.)

Ley D, 1974 "Problems of co-optation and idolatry in the community group" in *Community Participation and the Spatial Order of the City* Ed. D Ley (Tantalus Research, Vancouver)

Mishan E J, 1969 *Welfare Economics: Ten Introductory Essays* (Random House, New York)

Murphy H, Pennee B, Luchins D, 1972 "Foster homes: The new back wards?" *Canada's Mental Health* Supplement 71

Olson M, 1971 *The Logic of Collective Action* 2nd edition (Schocken Books, New York)

Rothenburg J, 1967 *Economic Evaluation of Urban Renewal* (Brookings Institution, Washington, DC)

Roweis S, 1975 "The land question and the analysis of suburbanization" paper presented at the 22nd Annual Meeting of the Regional Science Association, Cambridge, Mass.

Russo J R, 1974 "Mutually therapeutic interaction between mental patients and delinquents" *Hospital and Community Psychiatry* **25** 531-533

Schall L D, 1971 "A note on externalities and property valuation" *Journal of Regional Science* **XI** 101-105

Scott A J, 1975 "Land rent, land use, and transport: A study in the geographical foundations of political economy" Research Report, Joint Program in Transportation, University of Toronto

Seley J, 1973 *Paradigms and Dimensions of Urban Conflict* unpublished Ph D dissertation, University of Pennsylvania, Philadelphia

Staaf R, Tannian F, 1973 *Externalities: Theoretical Dimensions of Political Economy* (Dunellen Press, New York)

Teitz M B, 1968 "Toward a theory of urban public facility location" *Papers, Regional Science Association* **XXI** 38-51

Tiebout C M, 1956 "A pure theory of local expenditures" *Journal of Political Economy* **LXIV** 416-424

Titmuss R M, 1965 "Community care of the mentally ill: Some British observations" *Canada's Mental Health* Supplement 49

Weisbrod B A, 1965 "Geographic spillover effects and the allocation of resources to education" in *The Public Economy of Urban Communities* Ed. J Margolis (Resources for the Future, Washington, DC)

Williams O P, 1971 *Metropolitan Political Analysis* (Free Press, New York)

Williamson O, 1970 "Administrative decision-making and pricing: Externality and compensation analysis applied" in *The Analysis of Public Output* Ed. J Margolis (National Bureau of Economic Research, New York)

Wolpert J, Dear M, Crawford R, 1975 "Satellite mental health facilities" *Annals, Association of American Geographers* **65** 24-35 [Reprinted in *Ekistics* **40**(240) 342-347, 1975]

Wolpert J, Mumphrey A J, Seley J, 1972 "Metropolitan neighbourhoods: Participation and conflict over change" Resource Paper number 16, Commission on College Geography, Association of American Geographers, Washington, DC